The Extraordinary Life of A.A. Milne

Nadia Cohen

PEN & SWORD
HISTORY

First published in Great Britain in 2017 by
PEN AND SWORD HISTORY
an imprint of
Pen and Sword Books Ltd
47 Church Street
Barnsley
South Yorkshire S70 2AS

ISBN 978 1 52670 446 7

Printed and bound in the UK
by T J International, Padstow, Cornwall, PL28 8RW

Typeset in Times New Roman by
CHIC GRAPHICS

Pen & Sword Books Ltd incorporates the imprints of Pen & Sword
Archaeology, Atlas, Aviation, Battleground, Discovery,
Family History, History, Maritime, Military, Naval, Politics, Railways,
Select, Social History, Transport, True Crime, Claymore Press,
Frontline Books, Leo Cooper, Praetorian Press, Remember When,
Seaforth Publishing and Wharncliffe.

For a complete list of Pen and Sword titles please contact
Pen and Sword Books Limited
47 Church Street, Barnsley, South Yorkshire, S70 2AS, England
E-mail: enquiries@pen-and-sword.co.uk
Website: www.pen-and-sword.co.uk

Contents

Acknowledgements vii

Introduction viii

Chapter One   1
'It's always useful to know where a friend-and-relation is,
whether you want him or whether you don't.'

Chapter Two   13
'People who don't think probably don't have brains; rather,
they have grey fluff that's blown into their heads by mistake.'

Chapter Three   21
'Love is taking a few steps backward maybe even more…to
give way to the happiness of the person you love.'

Chapter Four   37
'The cold's so cold, and the hot's so hot.
Oh! God bless Daddy – I quite forgot.'

Chapter Five   47
'We will be friends until forever, just you wait and see.'

Chapter Six   62
'This writing business. Pencils and what-not. Over-rated, if
you ask me. Silly stuff. Nothing in it.'

Chapter Seven   69
'If there ever comes a day when we can't be together keep
me in your heart, I'll stay there forever.'

Chapter Eight   82
'If you live to be a hundred, I want to live to be a hundred
minus one day, so I never have to live without you.'

Chapter Nine   90
'You can't stay in your corner of the Forest waiting for others
to come to you. You have to go to them sometimes.'

Chapter Ten   96
'A day without a friend is like a pot without a single drop of
honey left inside.'

Chapter Eleven   105
'If the person you are talking to doesn't appear to be listening,
be patient. It may simply be that he has a small piece of fluff
in his ear.'

Chapter Twelve   121
'A little Consideration, a little thought for others, makes all the
difference.'

Chapter Thirteen   140
'It is hard to be brave, when you are only a Very Small Animal.'

Chapter Fourteen   156
'Just because an animal is large, it doesn't mean he doesn't want
kindness.'

Chapter Fifteen   169
'Promise me you'll never forget me because if I thought you
would I'd never leave.'

Chapter Sixteen   186
'How lucky I am to have something that makes saying goodbye
so hard.'

Bibliography   206

Dedication

For Harry and Felix

* * *

Acknowledgements

Thanks to my parents, Diana and Martin, for reading their original copies of Winnie-the-Pooh to me when I was a child, and always doing all the voices. And of course for their unswerving love, support and encouragement over the years.

Thank you also to the National Portrait Gallery, The Garrick Club and John Osborn for invaluable help with the picture research.

And to Dan Marsh for being far more patient than I deserved while I was writing this book.

Introduction

For many of us A.A. Milne's *Winnie-The-Pooh* stories need no introduction, since they have been loved by generations of children and their parents from the moment they were first published in 1926. They are so ingrained in our culture that certain sayings have become integral shorthand in family life. Growing up, we certainly included them in our daily rituals, sometimes asking for 'butter for the Royal slice of bread', or calling one another 'a bear of very little brain'.

It is a charming and harmless tradition I have enjoyed passing on to my own children. As twin boys their favourite quote, which even appears on their bedroom wall, comes from what we all agree is the most appropriate poem for them, Us Two which includes the line: 'Wherever I am there's always Pooh, there's always Pooh and Me.'

But despite the familiarity of his name, Alan Alexander Milne himself remains something of a mystery even now, sixty years after his death. A good deal of his most ardent readers do not realise that he also had a lengthy career as a successful playwright, screenwriter, novelist and was the brains behind countless humorous magazine articles. Fewer still know that he fought in the Battle of the Somme in the First World War and wrote propaganda pieces for the war effort as a member of a top-secret government unit called MI7b.

The youngest of three sons, he grew up in the boarding school where his father was the headmaster, and used many of the adventures he had with his older brother Ken as inspiration for his adorable literary creations. Others were based on stories he would tell his son Christopher Robin, who inspired the character of the same name.

Winnie-the-Pooh brought the author phenomenal fame and fortune, but made neither himself nor Christopher Robin happy. Alan died still seething with resentment that he was never taken as seriously as he would have wanted. He longed to be thought of as a thought-provoking and politically minded adult author, but no matter what else he wrote, he was permanently labelled as a whimsical children's storyteller. Whimsical was a word he grew to despise deeply over the years, just as his son grew to bitterly hate the fact that his childhood had been made public property without his consent.

Christopher felt that his father would never have come up with the ideas without him, although Alan did his best to share the credit with his son who adored his toy animals, as well as his wife Daphne who gave the characters their voices. And of course he owed a great debt to his illustrator E.H. Shepard who brought each scene so magically to life. In his autobiography Alan explained:

The animals in the stories came from the most part from the nursery. My collaborator (his wife Daphne) had already given them individual voices, their owner by constant affection had given them the twist in their features which denotes character, and Shepard drew them, as one might say, from the living model.

Despite the stories and books Alan wrote for children being so well known, the man himself was enigmatic. In many ways, of course, he is remembered as every inch the traditional English gentleman who smoked a pipe, played golf and could usually be found reading *The Times* in a leather wing-backed armchair at his private members club.

But there was much more to this troubled man who spent much of his life trying desperately to change perceptions about him. Following a first class education at Westminster School and Cambridge University, he started his career as a humourist writing sketches for the satirical magazine Punch. But for an ambitious man like him, that job was never going to enough and so he branched out into novels and plays, with some success.

His publishers complained furiously when he sent them a detective story, and objected even more bitterly when he announced that he had decided on a whim to write children's poetry. But his very first attempt, *When We Were Very Young*, turned out to be one of the best selling books of all time. It sold an astonishing 50,000 copies in the first eight weeks, and they soon stopped complaining when they saw the profits piling up! And now, almost a century after Winnie-the-Pooh was published, they still remain among the most popular and profitable children's characters, contributing to a global industry that rakes in millions of pounds every year.

But for the author, and his son, they became an almost intolerable burden.

He refused even the most lucrative offers for more children's stories, determined to focus on his plays, which he longed to have more widely appreciated. Meanwhile Christopher, famous almost from birth, endured vicious taunts and cruel bullying from other boys at school. He battled relentlessly against the perception that he must be that sweet little boy from the books. He felt his father exploited important moments from his childhood, and took all the credit for it, leaving him to fight his battles unsupported. Christopher said that by using his name, he had been deprived of his own identity, and wrote in his autobiography: 'He filched from me my good name and had left me with nothing but the empty fame of being his son.'

By the time the last children's book, *The House At Pooh Corner*, was published, irreparable damage had been done. Their relationship in adulthood was strained and uncomfortable. And when Christopher decided to marry his first cousin, leading to the birth of a badly handicapped child, a rift deepened between them which never healed. Daphne was heartbroken when her only son openly described his upbringing as cold and detached, revealing that his parents left much of his care to a nanny and boarding schools.

When Christopher told how his mother was often absent during his early years, the fall-out culminated in her demanding that a sculpture of her son was to be buried in the grounds of their Sussex home where she would never have to lay eyes on it again.

Yet Daphne and Alan remained devoted to each other, and she nursed him until the very end, having survived a turbulent period in their marriage when Daphne spent weeks at a time visiting her lover in New York. Alan appeared to know all about her romance with American playwright Elmer Rice, but once again proved himself ahead of his time by turning a blind eye He was also rumoured to be having an affair at the time, the subject of much scurrilous gossip among the theatrical community, with a young actress called Leonora Corbett who was often cast in his plays.

But even at the peak of his success, while appearing to revel in the glitz and glamour of moving among the highest social circles, Alan always had dark shadows cast over him. He never really stopped grieving for the loss of his older brother Ken who had been his closest friend and ally until his early death. Nor could he ever let go of his firmly held political opinions, which he often discussed in strongly worded letters to the newspapers. Haunted by the suffering he witnessed on the battlefields of the Somme in the First World War, he declared himself a pacifist in a time of great national patriotism and pride in the Armed Forces. When Adolf Hitler began to seize power in Germany in the 1930s and the threat of a second global conflict loomed on the horizon, Alan wrote an impassioned plea for peace. He was frustrated by politicians' inability to find a peaceful solution and *Peace With Honour* became one of his most challenging and widely read adult books.

But as the great man himself wrote in the introduction to Winnie-the–Pooh: 'And now all the others are saying, "What about Us?" So perhaps the best thing to do is to stop writing Introductions and get on with the book.'

CHAPTER ONE

'It's always useful to know where a friend-and-relation is, whether you want him or whether you don't.'

Very few authors can ever dream of coming close to the legacy left by A.A. Milne. He remains a household name in almost every corner of the globe thanks to a phenomenally popular collection of whimsical children's stories about an adorable little boy named Christopher Robin and his beloved teddy bear. Generations of children have grown up loving the tales of *Winnie-The-Pooh* and his friends from the Hundred Acre Wood, which are still among the most popular – and profitable – fictional characters in the world.

But while the poems and stories bring unparalleled joy to millions today, just as they did when they were first published almost a century ago, their creator Alan Alexander Milne himself was never able to fully enjoy the fame and fortune they brought him. He died deeply resenting *Winnie-the-Pooh*'s enormous success, since as far as he was concerned those stories were merely a tiny fraction of his literary work; yet no matter how hard he tried, nothing else he produced during his long and fascinating career as a playwright and political activist ever came close in terms of public appreciation.

Throughout his charmed life the author blatantly defied the rigid social rules of the day. He ignored widespread and scurrilous gossip about his unconventional marriage, as his wife spent weeks at a time with her lover in New York while he entertained actresses in London. During two world wars, in times of great patriotism and national pride, he brushed aside accusations of cowardice as he campaigned for peace, and he never recovered from the heartache of losing his adored older brother tragically young.

All the wealth and adulation meant nothing since the author never resolved a bitter feud with his only son, the real-life Christopher Robin, who accused him of exploiting his childhood for his own inspiration and profit. Just like his father, Christopher was unable to come to terms with the unique place he held in literary history. He felt he was never given a choice. After suffering vicious bullying throughout his teens he grew to loathe his famous family, and could not forgive Alan for destroying those precious early years.

Despite a long illness that left him confined to a wheelchair, even on his deathbed Alan simply could not reconcile the fact that no matter what else he wrote, regardless of all the plays and stories for adults he had published, he would always be remembered fondly – but simply – as a children's storyteller.

It has always been widely assumed that the famous tales were written about the imaginary adventures that his son had with his nursery toys, but it has now emerged that Alan actually drew much of the material from his own idyllic childhood. From the day he was born, on 18 January 1882 in Mortimer Road, North London, Alan Alexander was destined for literary success. He showed a remarkably advanced flair for writing from an extraordinarily young age, thanks to encouragement from his doting father John Vine Milne, the headmaster of Henley House, a small private boy's school in Hampstead. John was absolutely delighted by the arrival of the youngest of his three sons and took a particularly keen interest in Alan's early education. He was naturally gifted, and John was thrilled when the boy mastered reading at the age of $2^{1}/_{2}$ – way ahead of both his older brothers David Barrett and Kenneth John. 'In Papa's house it was natural to be interested,' Alan remarked years later. 'It was easy to be clever.'

Alan was originally named Alexander Sydney, but his father returned to the register office to make the change within weeks, after deciding to rename him after his own beloved uncle Alan, known as Ackie, who lived with the family at the time. The earliest photo that survives of Alan was taken in 1886 when he was just 4 years old. He is seated alongside his two brothers – all of them blonde, blue-eyed boys – and all three are dressed in black velvet suits, buttoned knickerbockers and large lace collars, with long curly hair. According to the tradition of the time, children's hair was not cut until they reached the age of 10, and Alan never forgot ceremoniously handing his flowing locks over to his mother Maria in a paper bag following his first haircut.

John Milne was a traditional father in many ways, urging his boys to be strong, independent and adventurous – he wanted 'manly little fellows' and Alan lived up to every expectation. He enjoyed the best of town and country life, since at that time Hampstead was at the very edge of London and a penny bus would take the boys from their street to the countryside of Cricklewood, where they were free to have adventures in just two short miles. A century ago Mortimer Road, which is now Mortimer Crescent, was a very respectable address. Indeed, the Milne's nearest neighbours included a solicitor, a stockbroker, and a retired colonel, as well as the political author Annie Bessant. Next door to Henley House was a convent, St Peter's House, home to twenty-five nuns and twenty-five girls, who were a constant source of fascination to the Milne boys! The illustrator E.H. Shepard, who would later bring the *Winnie-the-Pooh* tales so perfectly to life through his expressive drawings, was living just five minutes' walk away, but he and Alan did not meet and form their fruitful partnership until they were working together at the satirical magazine *Punch* many years later.

Henley House, which is now a block of flats run by Camden Council, was never just an ordinary family home. Looking back in 1939 Alan described it as: 'One of those private schools, then so common, now so unusual. For boys of all ages'. The 1881 census showed that there were thirteen boarders aged between 6 and 16 living at the school, one boy's parents were based in Paris, another came from as far as Montenegro Bay; coincidentally the Milne family also had strong connections to Jamaica since John had been born there, the eldest son of a Scottish Congregational Minister called William Milne, who met his wife Harriet Newell Barrett after travelling to Jamaica to work as a missionary. William, who Alan later called 'the world's most unworldly muddler', fathered ten children although his income never

3

went beyond eighty pounds a year, so the family lived exclusively on porridge and only four of the children survived to adulthood. By 1874 John had been sent back to England where he found work as an apprentice in an engineering firm, although he spent his evenings studying Latin and Greek in the hope of qualifying as a teacher. He achieved his goal and took a job at a boy's school in Shropshire, and as a keen flute player he would often attend musical evenings at a local girls' school where he met his future wife Sarah Maria Heginbotham, Alan's mother, who was always known as Maria.

John adored teaching, and always felt far more at ease with children than adults, although he looked so young that he had to grow a beard to help control his pupils who were often bigger than him. He was certainly one of the most popular members of staff, but his methods were controversial by the standards of the day and he landed himself in trouble at the Shropshire school when, just a week after the headmaster warned the boys that they would go to hell if they did not work hard, he told them there was no such place as hell and no everlasting fire. Not long after this scandal, John proposed to Maria, who turned him down initially. She was happily single and used to living alone, having had her heart broken by another man some years earlier. But John persisted, and eventually she accepted. John said: 'In my wife I had a wonderful gift', and in her only surviving letter, written when Alan got married and she was 73, Maria wrote a moving tribute to her own thirty-five happy years of 'well-chosen partnership'.

John and Maria married near her home in Buxton, Derbyshire, on 27 August 1878; John was 33 and Maria was already 38 years old, which at that time was considered late to marry and certainly rather old to start a family. Their first son Barry was born three-and-a-half years later, and Maria was well into her forties by the time Alan came along. Following their wedding, the couple moved down to London and took over Henley House from a man called John Leeds who had been running it unsuccessfully – with just nine boarders – and the Milnes reopened the school under new management in the autumn of 1878. John feared they had invested their life savings in 'twenty or thirty inky desks and half a dozen inky boys'.

CHAPTER ONE

It was a time before school regulation or inspections, so school owners were pretty much left to their own devices when it came to the curriculum, but if parents wanted their children to be educated beyond the compulsory leaving age of 12, they had no choice except to pay. The classical education offered by fee-paying grammar schools was already being seen as old fashioned, and private schools like Henley House attempted to plug the gaps in secondary education.

Alan took great inspiration from his hard-working father, and friends of the family would later draw many comparisons between John and his son's famously wise and thoughtful character Owl. When Owl made his first appearance in *Winnie-The-Pooh*, Alan wrote: "'And if anyone knows anything about anything," said Bear to himself, "It's Owl who knows something about something. Or my name's not Winnie the Pooh," he said. "Which it is.'" While both wore a traditional schoolmaster's cap and gown, John was not pretentious or pedantic like Owl, and never used long words in a bid to impress. And unlike Owl, John had a great sense of humour. His middle son Ken was just 3 years old when he apparently said that his father had 'too much laugh' for a schoolteacher.

Pupils arriving at Henley House found John was most unusual in his teaching methods, since he preferred to think of exams as 'not tests of what a boy has learnt, but intended to make him think'. He would ask the boys to name things in the world that appeared most beautiful, and the reply that delighted him most was 'a boy with a smiling countenance'. It was a happy school and when prizes were awarded, John made sure every boy who got more than seventy-five per cent of the possible marks received a prize: 'There was no danger of emulation becoming envy,' he insisted. And when his sons were toddlers he would perch them on a table to hand out the pupils' prizes: 'Without affection the schoolroom is a hard, forbidding place. With love, it becomes the next best place to home', John said. Clearly Henley House was an unconventional school in many ways, the most notable being that John did not bother with many of the strict rules that governed other Victorian establishments at the time. He once surprised his pupils by announcing: 'You will find no rule, for instance, that you may not put soup down your neighbour's back, or that you may not go to church in your football dress'. Discipline was reserved for more important things – he could not stand lying, cheating or bullying.

Although John said that the boys would always go to their mother first when they needed comfort, Alan adored his father, and never enjoyed quite such a close relationship with Maria. Years later when he came to write about his parents, Alan said:

> *He was the best man I have ever known; by which I mean the most truly good, the most completely to be trusted, the most incapable of wrong. He differed from our conception of God only because he was shy, which one imagined God not to be, and was funny, which we knew God was not. As a child I gave my heart to my father. We loved Mama too, though not so dearly. I don't think I ever really knew her.*

And when summing up his relationship with his mother, he explained:

> *A mother's job is not to prevent wounds, but to bind up the wounded. She had the Victorian woman's complete faith in the rights of a father. It was he who was bringing us up. He conceded her the Little Lord Fauntleroy make-up and did his best to nullify its effect.*

After Alan was born, there would be no more children for the Milnes, although John longed for a girl, as he admitted in 1928: 'My only regret was that we had no daughters. But my wife used to say, "Sons are good enough for me."'

Maria remained very much in the background throughout Alan's childhood. Although she was an excellent cook and artist – her schoolgirl tapestry of *The Last Supper* remains intact – Alan and his brothers appeared to have thought little of her and she does not seem to appear in his work. The most memorable female character that Alan created was Kanga, Roo's sensible mother, who did very little apart from scold the other animals and dish out Extract of Malt, known as

Strengthening Medicine. The various other women who appear in Alan's poems were based on either his somewhat frivolous wife Daphne de Selincourt, or Christopher Robin's nanny Olive Rand. Like Kanga, Maria was unemotional and not easily upset. She left most of the childcare to her husband who was responsible for educating and disciplining them. The boys recalled many happy memories of hiking with their father during long summer holidays spent in the idyllic Shropshire countryside. Maria made sure she had her way with the children's clothes and their hair, but her influence did not reach far beyond that, and Alan had very few memories involving his mother: 'When I was a child I neither experienced nor felt the need of, the mother-love of which one reads so much and over which I am supposed so mistakenly, to have sentimentalised', he said later.

As was common at the time, Maria employed a nanny, Beatrice Edwards, to help with the children, and the boys were utterly devoted to her. They called her Bee, and before becoming a pupil at Henley House, Alan was under her watchful eye almost constantly. She slept in his bedroom at home, and each morning she walked him to Wykeham House nursery school. Alan enjoyed his days at the small school, which was run by sisters Alice and Florence Budd, and he won several prizes for his writing which was outstanding from a very young age. Bee would read him his favourite stories, *Uncle Remus* and *Reynard The Fox*, and when he later came to read for himself, Alan loved *Treasure Island* and *The Swiss Family Robinson,* which encouraged his love of the outdoor life and desert islands – he later said his best holidays had been to small islands including the Orkneys, Sicily and Capri.

Just like the happy characters he later created, Alan's world was more influenced by nannies and nursery rules than his actual parents, and his priorities were friendship, hunger and a desire for adventure. For much of their childhood Alan and his older brother Ken shared a long-running fantasy that they would wake up one morning and find that everyone else in the world was dead. Each night after lights out they would embellish the fantasy – imagining themselves stepping over Bee's lifeless body, thrilled that there was nobody to ask if they had washed. After checking there were no others survivors, they planned to sneak out and explore the world. They imagined helping themselves at local sweet shops, and driving a horse bus – since animals were always spared their fictitious plague. Alan and Ken were never particularly close to their eldest brother Barry who was rarely involved in their games, since he was often absent from home for long periods; suffering from a series of childhood illnesses he was sent to convalesce from Scarlet Fever at a farm in Hendon.

Although Alan and Ken dreamt longingly of freedom, they actually had a great deal of independence, and spent their time roaming fields, forests, cricket pitches and golf courses. 'Almost as babies, we were allowed to go for walks by ourselves anywhere, in London or in the country,' Alan recalled. As a young boy he was happiest when it was just him and Ken, as they shared everything:

We were inseparable, Alan said. Sometimes, when fighting, so mixed up as to be indistinguishable. We never ceased to quarrel with each other, nor to feel the need of each other. Save for the fact that he hated cheese, we shared equally all belief, all knowledge, all ambition, all hope and all fear.

The two boys usually chose to share a bed, but they would fight every morning: 'When one of us found the tide of clothes had receded in the night, leaving him bare and beached'. If it was not a school day they would usually wake early, grab handfuls of porridge oats from the kitchen if the family cook was not yet up, and sneak out of the house before anybody realised they had gone. They both agreed that breakfast was the best meal of the day, and Alan would later write:

"When you wake in the morning Pooh," said Piglet at last, "what's the first thing you say to yourself?" "What's for breakfast?" said Pooh. "What do you say Piglet?" "I say, I wonder what's going to happen exciting today?" said Piglet. Pooh nodded thoughtfully. "It's the same thing," he said.

CHAPTER ONE

Since they could not fulfil their secret shared fantasy of being dead, early morning adventures were the next best thing to Alan and Ken. Knowing they would not be in trouble unless they woke their parents up, they once bowled iron hoops for miles, but were back in time for breakfast. Another day they got up at 5.30am and had a fight with long bamboo poles, a present from Jamaica, which hung in the hall. Despite their great adventures, which were followed, if they were lucky, with plates of their favourite meal of ham and eggs, they were never late for classes, and Alan particularly took his studies seriously.

Although they took quite different paths in later life, they remained the best of friends until Ken's early death. After he passed away, Alan admitted that his success had often been tough for Ken:

All through Ken's schooldays it was a reproach to him that his younger brother was intellectually his superior, Alan said. But Ken had one advantage of me. He was definitely nicer, kinder, larger-hearted, more loveable, more tolerant, sweeter tempered. If you knew us both, you preferred Ken. I might be better at work and games; even better looking but poor old Ken, or dear old Ken, had his private right of entry into everybody's heart.

If, in later years, I have not seemed insufferable to my friends over any success which has looked in on me, I owe it to him, in whose company complacence found nothing on which to batten. And if I have taken failure less well than I should have done, it is because I am still sixteen months behind him in humility, and shall never catch up.

As well as their private adventures, there were outings for the whole family too. A trip to see a production of *Beauty and the Beast* gave Alan an early taste of the theatre, which would later come to dominate his life as he found fame as a playwright. He was entranced by his first show in London's West End: 'I just gazed and gazed at Beauty,' he recalled. 'Never had I seen anything so lovely. For weeks afterwards I dreamed about her. Nothing that was said or done on the stage mattered so long as she was there'.

Even then he realised that the children in the audience were probably not listening to the dialogue, but instead waiting for something to happen, or for their favourite character to return. This rare insight into children's minds would later serve him so well. Alan also found himself drawn to the popular Victorian musical halls, which he first experienced on holiday in Ramsgate with a somewhat disreputable relative known only as Cousin Anne who worked in a shop in London's South Audley Street, and introduced the three Milne boys to the power of what was known as 'cheap music'. Alan was also taken on exciting excursions by his Uncle Ackie and Aunt Mary – who later appeared as Aunt Alice in a poem describing a happy visit to the Crystal Palace. He distinctly remembered a feeling of pure joy on those outings: 'Childhood,' he wrote, 'is not the happiest time of one's life, but only to a child is pure happiness possible'. Alan adored Ackie and Mary, who worked with his parents at Henley House and after his uncle died, Alan described him as 'the best and bravest of men'.

It has been widely assumed that that all the material in *When We Were Very Young*, Alan's first collection of children's poetry, was inspired by the childhood of his own son Christopher Robin, but Alan has since admitted that he actually drew on 'a combination of memory, observation and imagination'. And in his introduction to *Very Young Verses*, published in 1929, he confirmed: 'Some of the things in these books were things I remembered doing myself years and years ago. As a child I played lines-and-squares in a casual sort of way. Christopher Robin never did until he read what I had written about it, and not very enthusiastically then'. Alan later remembered Barry teasing him for playing that game which has since become loved by generations of children.

Shortly after his seventh birthday, during his first term as a pupil at Henley House, Alan gave his first public performance, alongside Ken, in a Christmas concert held at Kilburn Town Hall, playing classical music by Mozart. Among the audience was H.G. Wells, who went on to write science fiction novels including *The War of the Worlds*. He had just joined the school as a teacher, took a shine to Alan and became a lifelong friend and mentor. In a glowing profile which appeared in the Henley House school magazine, Wells wrote about his favourite pupil:

He does not like French – does not see that you prove anything when you have done. Thinks mathematics grand. He leaves his books about; loses his pen; can't imagine what he did with this, and where he put that, but is convinced that it is somewhere. Clears his brain when asked a question by spurting out some nonsense, and them immediately after gives a sensible reply.

Can speak 556 words per minute, and writes more in three minutes than his instructor can speak in thirty. Finds this a very interesting world, and would like to learn physiology, botany, geology, astronomy and everything else. Wishes to make a collection of beetles, bones, butterflies etc., and cannot determine whether Algebra is better than football or Euclid than a sponge cake.

The other dignitary at the classical concert was Lord Alfred Harmsworth, who had been the first editor of the Henley House magazine in the term that Alan was born. As a teenager he was drifting ineffectually through school when John Milne took him under his wing and encouraged him to produce a mock newspaper. Alfred seized the challenge with great relish, and saw to it that the first professionally printed issue of the *Henley House School Magazine* bore the words 'Edited By Alfred Harmsworth' in large bold type. It was an early indication of the shape of things to come, as that early taste for journalism led him to eventually become a millionaire media mogul who owned the *Daily Mail, Daily Mirror* and *The Times* newspapers, among others. Alfred had fond memories of the school he attended with his three brothers, and enjoyed the show so much that evening that he invited the boys to visit Penshurst, his sprawling estate in the Kent countryside. Alan never forgot that holiday, because it was when he acquired his first pet, a Gordon Setter dog called Brownie who inspired one of his very first poems *Puppy and I*. The

Milne brothers may have had their differences, but all the boys were united in how much they adored Brownie, who had been abandoned for being gun shy, and would hide under the table at the sound of thunder. Brownie, who was later described in the famous poem as 'a heaven-sent gift', fitted into the family perfectly as they were all rather shy in public too.

Alan later fell out with the newspaper baron whom he blamed for declining standards in the industry: 'He killed the penny dreadful (newspaper) by the simple process of producing a halfpenny dreadfuller,' he said. But he also had Harmsworth to thank for publishing what is thought to be one of his earliest surviving pieces of prose, which he wrote for the school magazine. Entitled '*My Three Days Walking Tour* by Alan A. Milne Aged 8 ¾'. He wrote: 'After a little while it cleared up, and we walked to Ashdown Forest, where it again poured with rain. As it was so wet, we were not able to go through the forest, which was mostly a common, six or seven miles long and three miles broad'.

Thirty-six years later Alan vividly recalled each and every delightful detail of that particularly memorable hike, as Ashdown Forest in Sussex was to become not only his home, but also the inspiration for the Hundred Acre Wood.

CHAPTER TWO

'People who don't think probably don't have brains; rather, they have grey fluff that's blown into their heads by mistake.'

John Milne wanted little more than to provide the very best education for his boys, and to his mind, Westminster School in London was the finest establishment in the country in the summer of 1892. He had his sights set on winning scholarships for all three of his sons, although Ken was mortified when he was the first brother to be sent up for the Challenge – as the entrance exam was known – wearing knickerbockers, alongside fifty-two other boys who were all wearing long trousers.

Despite the sartorial embarrassment, Ken qualified for a place, but did not win the scholarship, and neither did Barry, who was packed off to a private school in Derbyshire. And so it was left to Alan to fulfil his father's dream. There was a lot to learn, but Ken, who found the school tough and lonely at first, would come home at weekends to help coach his eager younger brother. With Ken's help, he learnt all the school's strange jargon like 'bag' for milk, 'beggar' for sugar and 'blick' for ball: 'You couldn't say that it must be wrong because it was silly, but rather you had to say, "That must be right because people have been doing it for three hundred years,"' said Alan who was determined to say and do whatever it took to be reunited with Ken again, they could not bear to be apart much longer.

When he took the Westminster Challenge papers, his Greek was disastrous but his outstanding mathematics score more than made up for it, and when he became the youngest ever Queen's Scholar, his father was delighted. The money they saved on Alan's fees meant all the boys were given new bicycles for Christmas that year, and they were able to rent a holiday home in Westgate-on-Sea.

During his first term at Westminster, Alan struck up close bonds with boys who would remain his friends for life, but he was confused by all the rules, the maze of buildings, and the lack of basic hygiene – he was horrified to learn that there were no baths and no hot water. When the boys came in muddy from games they were given a jug of cold water each, and had to stand shivering in a shallow tin bath in an attempt to get clean again before lessons.

Alan also hated the food, and for the rest of his life could 'not think of college meals without disgust and indignation'. For breakfast, which had always been his favourite meal, Alan was utterly bewildered to be served with meagre rations of bread and unsalted butter, which he described as 'inferior Vaseline – the sort of thing you put on the axles of locomotives'. He was constantly ravenous, and complained:

The milk had been boiled, and great lumps of skin floated about on the top of it. It made me almost sick to look at that milk, to smell that milk, to think of that milk. I lay awake every night thinking about food, he said. I fell asleep and dreamed about food. In all my years at Westminster I never ceased to be hungry.

And yet his empty stomach growling with hunger was not the worst indignity for Alan. What he feared most was being 'tanned'. Corporal punishment was an everyday occurrence in schools at the time, which came as a particularly nasty shock to Alan after the family atmosphere of Henley House where his father found the idea of hitting a child 'utterly distasteful'. But at Westminster a tanning meant being thrashed four times with a thick cane, and Alan described the constant fear he endured as 'such an unnecessary hardship'. For the rest of his life he could never understand anyone approving of corporal punishment. He wrote: 'The curious, but not infrequent boast "Thrashing never did me any harm," invites the retort: "Then what did?"'

Despite all this, Alan made a good start at Westminster and in his report at the end of his first term the headmaster described him as: 'Keen, intelligent and improving fast'. Maths ended up being his best subject, although he struggled with it at first, and was so bad at French he usually resorted to cheating. He and Ken regularly deceived their father about how they spent each term's £5 pocket money, and during lessons they wrote each other long letters making plans for the holidays, having developed their own secret code – leaving out alternate words for the other to fill in the blanks.

Huge emphasis was placed on sport at Westminster, and luckily Alan was a keen athlete – he was one of the fastest sprinters and won prizes for the long jump. He also developed his love of golf at school, but one of his proudest moments was being selected for the school's cricket team, and he wrote in detail about how devastated he was in the summer of 1899, when he was bowled out without scoring a single run in an important two-day match against arch-rivals Charterhouse School. It sparked a life-long passion for the game, which he would always share with Ken, and later Christopher Robin; at the end of his life Alan said that watching cricket had given him 'more happiness than any other inactivity in which I have been engaged'.

Westminster did remarkably little to prepare Alan for his career as a writer however, English Literature was barely taught at the time, and with very little importance placed on writing in the classroom; boys had to wait until their sixth year before they could join the Literary Society and read fiction. Alan said that in seven years he did not write one essay and left not knowing 'whether Milton lived before or after Shakespeare'.

But Alan loved reading and most evenings he would take himself off to the school library for an hour, it was there he discovered the works of Charles Dickens and Jane Austen – *Pride and Prejudice* always remained one of his favourite books and he dramatised it more than forty years later. Boys were forbidden from taking books out of the library but Alan would often slip them inside his waistcoat on a Friday, spend much of Sunday reading, and return the book on a Monday before anyone noticed it had gone.

Holidays were spent at the family's new house in Westgate-on-Sea, cycling, riding horses and playing cricket and croquet on the lawn. They also kept ducks, bees, and even a peacock in the vast seven-acre gardens, which were a welcome change for the boys after the cramped school playgrounds and dormitories. They missed the place so much during term time that Maria would send her sons boxes of flowers from the garden, which Alan said brought with them 'a nostalgia almost unbearable'.

When he was 16 the family embarked on a rare foreign holiday, taking a cruise to Norway, where Alan experienced his first feelings for a girl on board, and wrote:

When she sat swinging her legs on the deck rail, gaily holding her own against all our compliments, mine wordless but by far the most sincere; when at moments she caught my eye and she gave me that warm sudden smile which meant that we two had some secret which the others did not share; then I felt that I could have died for her, or thrown my cap overboard (though I was more doubtful about this) if she had desired it.
Was I in love for the first time? I don't know.

Years later, in 1940, he wrote again about his teenage crush, calling the girl Matilda:

We reached Stavanger. Did I shout?
Behold Stavanger! Key to Norway?
I did not. No I lay in wait
In sight of Cabin 28
And caught Matilda coming out
And kissed her in the doorway.

Not every holiday was filled with such happy memories however; the Christmas of 1899 was an uncomfortable one for Alan as he was sent home from school in disgrace, not knowing whether or not he was going to be expelled when he returned after the break. He had been caught drinking and smoking as he celebrated the last night of school production of Terence's *Adelphi*, along with the rest of the cast. As he was left to sweat it out until the New Year, his future looked uncertain because he had also failed, despite all the expectations, to win a maths scholarship to Cambridge University. But that was also the holiday when he realised that his talents lay elsewhere and perhaps a very different career to the one mapped out for him could lie ahead. Alan met a family friend, a teenage girl known only as Ghita, who asked him to help her improve on a poem she was trying to write for Ken. He looked at what she had come up with so far, and immediately knew he could do better: 'The theme, one of cheerful insult, was good, but the execution was poor,' he recalled. 'I took some of the bones out, moderated the scansion and arranged for a few rhymes.' It was possibly the first time Alan experienced writing for pleasure and, after admitting to his brother that the poem had not actually come from Ghita, he and Ken realised they had discovered a new hobby and spent the next two years enthusiastically exchanging light-hearted verses between Westminster and Weymouth on the Dorset coast, where by now Ken was studying to become a solicitor.

Luckily, the drinking and smoking was forgiven by the headmaster, and Alan was allowed to return to school in time for his eighteenth birthday, when he happened to show a copy of *Granta*, the Cambridge undergraduate magazine, to his great friend Arthur Gaye who said: 'You ought to go to Cambridge and edit that,' and Alan apparently replied: 'I will'.

'It had an heroic sound,' he said later. 'But to anybody who has said "I can do it" at the age of two, saying "I will" at the age of eighteen is easy.'

With Ken gone, Alan worked much harder that term, he became a key member of the school debating team, and this time he succeeded in winning a scholarship to Trinity College, Cambridge. He was glad when the time came to leave in the summer of 1900, having been 'a Westminster boy for far too long'. Although he did not send his own son there, Alan always maintained his affection for the school, paying the fees when Ken's two sons became pupils, and returning to watch various drama productions. And while there were no masters he would remember as fondly as H.G. Wells, who inspired his love of writing, before he died he made Westminster one of the four beneficiaries of his will. The school inherited a share of the hugely lucrative rights to *Winnie-the-Pooh*, which were also divided between his family, the Royal Literary Fund, and the Garrick Club in London.

Alan thoroughly enjoyed his years at Cambridge. He quickly settled into at his rooms in Whewell Court and joined a crowd of former Westminster pupils, including Lytton Strachey and Saxon Sydney-Turner who stayed lifelong friends – they would all share a love of crossword puzzles when they were invented twenty years later.

During his time university Alan wrote many verses about love and courtship, mentioning several girls he was thought to have dated, with names including Clarissa, Dahlia, Myra, and Celia. One of the first poems he had published under his own name was called *In Case Of Rejection – What to do when a marriage proposal fails.* Together with Ken, he had come up with a set of comic 'instructions' for their potential wives including:

1. All women are beautiful: some are more beautiful than others: candidates for admission must be more beautiful than others.
2. All women are young: some are younger than others: candidates for admission must be younger than others.
3. All ladies are ready to oblige: some are readier than others: those who consent to write their names in this book will be readier than most.

And a few months later, during Alan's second year at university, Ken found a woman worthy of his proposal, Maud Innes, the sixth daughter of a Weymouth builder, but Alan remained single and appeared to be making the most of his bachelor years: 'We were very young in those days, laughing too easily, too loudly. Life for us was not rather a problem and at twenty most to be enjoyed,' he said.

After 'seven years of starvation' at Westminster, Alan also took great pleasure from being allowed to order pretty much whatever he wanted to eat at mealtimes, and never forgot the first moment he tasted Crème Brule, which always remained his favourite dessert. When he was not studying, Alan happily passed his spare time playing football for the college and appearing in plays. He became a keen member of the Shakespeare Society and the college debating club Magpie and Stump. He bought himself two silver bound pipes, and remained a pipe smoker for the rest of his life. He realised that he was never a great intellectual when it came to his chosen subject of mathematics, but felt more optimistic than ever that he could make a living as a writer. Alan barely opened some of the textbooks that filled his shelves, and admitted that his supervisor, a Scottish don called Gilbert Walker, did not see as much of him as he would have liked.

Alan and Ken bombarded *Granta* with their jointly written poems in a bid to supplement Alan's student income, as he often complained of being broke. His father sent each of his sons £100 a year, in instalments, which should have been plenty of money but Alan felt it was never quite enough. At the time the editor of *Granta* was Edwin Montagu, who later claimed to have discovered Milne's talents, although he turned down many of his early efforts: 'I remember how I rejected – how arrogant we were – his first contributions, telling him to persevere and that he might one day learn to write,' said Montagu.

To Alan's amazement some of his verses, *Sonnets of Love*, were accepted during his second term at Cambridge, three weeks later his first piece of prose appeared, and from then on a steady stream of his contributions, many of them jointly written with Ken, were published. Alan was thrilled when he stopped off in a pub in Bletchley on the way back from a football match one evening, and overheard the team captain saying: 'Did you see those awfully good verses in *Granta* this week – a sort of limerick by somebody called AKM?' Alan, glowing with pride, said: 'If only Ken had been next to me, so that we could have nudged each other and grinned, and talked it over happily together afterwards'. Their fruitful long-distance writing partnership continued well into Alan's second year but the brothers' last joint poem appeared in June 1902, since that summer Ken decided to withdraw from their arrangement as he embarked on his legal career: 'His reason was that I could do this sort of thing perfectly well without him,' Alan explained simply. 'His heart wasn't in frivolity, he wanted to be more serious'.

It was only a minor setback; to Alan's amazement, at Easter 1902 he received a rambling twenty-page letter from Clement Jones, who had taken over from Edwin Montagu as the new editor of *Granta*, asking if he wanted the top job at the magazine. He leapt at the opportunity, lured not only by the publication's impressive history, but also its long-running connections to the popular satirical magazine *Punch*, which was where his ultimate ambitions lay. His college tutor warned Alan that the job would not leave sufficient time for his studies, and threatened to withdraw his academic funding, but Alan was determined to find enough hours in the day to succeed at both and threw himself wholeheartedly into his first editorship.

John Milne was becoming increasingly concerned that his youngest son seemed to be devoting himself to the magazine at the expense of his studies, and rightly so as Alan barely scraped through to graduation in the summer of 1903 with low marks and a third-class degree: 'Father was so bitterly disappointed that for a week he did not talk to me,' he said. John held out hope that Alan might take a steady job with the civil service, and perhaps end up with a knighthood one day. Alan dutifully went along to a history crammer course, but John could see that his heart was not in it and urged his son to become a schoolteacher instead. He suggested a year in Germany to study the latest educational methods, before returning to Streete Court School in Westgate-on-Sea, which John was running by that time and imagined Alan would take over when he retired. But Alan knew a career in teaching was not for him, and after breaking the bad news to his father, he wrote decisively to his mentor H.G. Wells: 'I am going to try my luck at journalism. I know this sounds very foolish, but I believe it is better to go the whole hog rather than to pretend to be a school master during the term, and play at journalism in the holidays'.

A series of funny stories he had written called *Jeremy, I and the Jellyfish* caught the attention of R.C. Lehmann, the editor of *Punch*. Lehmann wrote to Alan, describing the stories as 'a piece of sparkling and entirely frivolous and irresponsible irrelevance', which led to the pair striking up a friendship that would prove invaluable. In 1924, shortly before the publication of his first children's verses, *When We Were Very Young*, Alan looked back on those golden opportunities at the start of his career and remarked: 'Does any of that divine youth hang over us still? If it be so, let us thank Cambridge and the *Granta* for casting the spell on us'.

CHAPTER THREE

'Love is taking a few steps backward maybe even more… to give way to the happiness of the person you love.'

Full of confidence and optimism about making his mark on the world of satirical journalism, A.A. Milne left Cambridge at the age of 21 and moved down to London in the autumn of 1903. He enthusiastically fired off a series of comedy sketches and dispatched them to the editor of *Punch*, but heard nothing back for seven months.

Alan's father was providing him with an allowance of £320 a year for living expenses, but it did not stretch very far, and there were certainly times when he wished he had followed John's well-meaning advice and taken a steady job in the civil service, tried his hand at teaching or even started at the bottom of the journalism ladder on a local newspaper: 'I often wish I had started as a reporter,' he would later reply to a fan letter. 'It is all experience for subsequent books and plays.'

He was living in two rooms in Bouverie Street, where breakfast was provided and all his laundry was taken care of. Most evenings he would dine at The Cock pub on Fleet Street, but several times a week he would catch a train out to Ealing for supper with Ken and his new wife Maud, who married in 1905 at St Paul's Church in Portman Square. Unusually for men of their generation, Alan and Ken would often cook together, and shared a fondness for cherry brandy. Maud was like a sister to Alan, and she encouraged his writing ambitions, urging him to send sketches off to all the evening papers.

He tried pulling a few strings, and contacted his father's former pupil Alfred Harmsworth, although the friendship had become strained a few years earlier when John had asked Harmsworth for a loan to secure the lease on Streete Court, and he had refused. His parents disapproved of Alan going to Harmsworth for help again but he needed work, although he later regretted getting back in touch: 'Like a fool I wrote to Harmsworth and the result made me very sick for a bit,' he said. Harmsworth passed his letter on to the literary editor of the *Daily Mail*, and Alan felt obliged to submit something:

> *I think I can say truthfully that those are the only words I have ever written which I did not write for my own pleasure. At the four hundredth word, I stopped, read them through, and with a sigh of happiness tore them into pieces. I was back on my own again, making, as Harmsworth said, my own way.*

His first solo poem eventually appeared in *Punch* on 18 May 1904, called *The New Game*, it only earned him a few pounds and a meagre income meant he had to move to cheaper rooms at 8 Wellington Square, Chelsea, which was a far less fashionable part of town at that time. He also reacquainted himself with his old teacher H.G. Wells who proved a great influence, socially and politically. Wells took Alan along to the National Liberal Club and suggested he find himself a literary agent as he was starting work on his first novel, *Lovers in London*. It was published in March 1905, leading to his first prose appearance in *Punch* – a popular series of sketches featuring Lilian, the main character from the book. But it was widely panned by critics and Alan was so embarrassed that he eventually bought back his copyright to prevent a reprint.

He was slowly starting to make a name for himself, but money was still tight, and that summer Alan felt obliged to take a short-term job in the Orkney Islands tutoring a boy who had missed some schooling. The wild scenery and time away from London made him long for the sort of adventures he and Ken had enjoyed as boys and inspired a second play, as well as several newspaper articles about his rural pursuits.

Back in London his writing appeared to be lacking impact and, by February 1906, Alan found himself sitting on a bench in Battersea Park seriously weighing up the options for his future: 'At twenty-four,' he thought, 'one must be certain of fame at thirty'. He doubted whether he would ever manage to get one of his plays produced, or make a name for himself in journalism. The only possibility, Alan felt, was to write a proper novel, which would somehow become the talk of London. He told his boss at *Punch*, Owen Seaman, that he would not be sending any more contributions for a few months as he was going to stay with his parents in the country, to write free from any distractions. His parents had recently retired from Streete Court to a nearby village called Steeple Bumpstead and Alan planned to stay with them while he came up with a brilliant novel that would establish him on the literary scene. But what Alan did not realise was that the editor F.C. Burnand had just been fired after twenty-six years, and Seaman was about to take the top job at *Punch*: 'He said he needed someone to relieve him of the worst of the donkey work: somebody who came in for, say, a couple of afternoons a week and sorted out the contributions,' Alan recalled. He was offered £250 a year for the role of Assistant Editor, with the golden opportunity of doubling it with his own contributions:

> *I tried to look grateful, eager, but not surprised, while doing simple arithmetic in my head, he said. Hadn't I always said that I would be Editor of Punch one day? Or hadn't I? I couldn't remember. Anyhow I was going to be.*
>
> *I wanted to think of all that it would mean, of all that I would write to Father, of all that I would tell Ken, but I could not think for happiness. Just as it seemed wonderful to be editing Granta after so short a struggle, so it seemed wonderful now to be, at twenty-four, Assistant Editor of Punch.*

He was right to feel so proud of himself, although he would later play it down, saying: 'My real achievement was to be not wholly the wrong person in the right place at the right time'.

Alan quickly settled into his new life at *Punch*, often spending weekends with his new friend Rudie Lehmann, playing tennis and boating at Fieldhead, his family's beautiful country mansion on the Thames in Berkshire. The tranquility of the house inspired Alan to write and Lehmann became a much closer friend than the main editor Seaman – who was said to have inspired the gloomy character of Eeyore the donkey. Seaman was a Conservative who clashed with Alan's Left-leaning politics, and often missed the publication's Friday afternoon deadlines which meant they were both kept in the office until the early hours on a Saturday morning. The job was demanding, but Alan loved it, and his social calendar was becoming very full. In May 1908 he was invited to take his place at the famous Punch Table, where the top writers and editors sat, and carved a neat monogram of his initials into the wood. An increased salary meant he could afford a better address, and he moved to rooms in Queen Anne's Gate near St James's Park which gave him a rich seam of material to mine for new a series of comedy sketches called *Bachelor Days*, about a young man in thrall to his bossy housekeeper: 'Of course, it is quite possible to marry for love,' he wrote, 'but I suspect that a good many bachelors marry so that they may not have to bother about the washing any more. That, anyhow, will be one of the reasons with me'. Around that time Alan gave up playing football for Westminster Old Boys, and took up golf instead as it was not so dirty. He fell passionately in love with his new hobby and wrote many jokes about it, including: 'Why do I hit the ball with a ridiculous club like this? I could send it father with a cricket bat. I could push it straighter with a billiard cue'.

Spending time with Ken and Maud, and now their young children Marjorie, Angela, and Ian, was a constant source of delight for Alan, and he dedicated *The Day's Play* to his eldest niece, whom he always called Margery. But Alan was also starting to meet influential members of society, and struck up a new friendship with E.V. Lucas, a writer at *Punch* who went on to become chairman of Methuen in the year that it published *When We Were Very Young*. Alan was a popular party guest at their country home in Lewes, and their friendship lasted many decades to come; Lucas's daughter later described him as 'glamorous'. They were both keen cricketers and Lucas introduced Alan to J.M. Barrie's famous literary cricket team The Allahakbarries. The *Peter*

Pan author was delighted by the introduction and when Alan sent him a copy of *The Day's Play*, Barrie replied: 'I feel an affection for the man behind your book, and hope all will always be well with you. Perhaps someday you will lunch with me. I wander about alone'.

Invitations came pouring in, and Alan found himself at fancy dress parties and lavish dinners with the likes of Winston Churchill, Raymond Asquith, and George Llewellyn Davies. He was still a bachelor and suggested, in August 1909, that falling in love was overrated: 'I should hate to be settled. It's so much more fun like this'. But the following December he was taken by Owen Seaman to a dance to celebrate the twenty-first birthday of his goddaughter Dorothy de Selincourt, and Alan knew he had met the one. Dorothy was very beautiful, but when asked to explain the initial attraction between them, Alan said: 'She laughed at my jokes'. She also endeared herself by showing that she knew some of his *Punch* pieces by heart.

Dorothy, who preferred to be known as Daphne or Daff, was born in Battersea on 2 November 1889, part of a large, wealthy and influential family; at first she and Alan were just friends. Neither of them was ready to settle down. Alan was thoroughly enjoying his new-found notoriety – in 1912 his name appeared in *Who's Who* for the first time – and as an eligible man about town, he certainly had no interest in getting married.

It was not until early January 1913 that he and Daphne crossed paths again, when they happened to find themselves buying ski boots together. By happy coincidence they were both going to the same resort in Switzerland, and glamorous Daphne was easy to spot on the slopes in her bright orange trousers. Alan was smitten, and proposed one morning in a snowstorm. Returning to London, he announced their engagement in the pages of *Punch* by writing: 'There are engagements and Swiss engagements – just as there are measles and German measles. It is well known that Swiss engagements don't count'.

But this one did, the couple were immediately overwhelmed with congratulations, and set about planning their big day. On 4 June 1913 Alan and Daphne were married in a large society wedding at St Margaret's Church in Westminster, with Alan's school friend Roland

Kitson as best man and Ken's daughters as bridesmaids. For their honeymoon the newlyweds spent three peaceful weeks on Dartmoor in Devon, before returning to their first marital home at 15 Embankment Gardens, London. Alan was devoted to Daphne and felt very lucky to be with her: 'If women only married men who were good enough for them,' he wrote, 'where should we be?' Before long they treated themselves to a second honeymoon at Cap Martin in the south of France where Alan found himself inspired to write a long-running series of pieces about the adventures of a family of rabbits, with the couple called Celia and Ronald widely assumed to be based on Daphne and Alan.

There was a great deal the pair did not know about each other when they married, and Daphne was completely innocent when it came to the physical side of their relationship, making her very nervous about any intimacy, having witnessed how badly her own mother suffered as a result of her father's wandering eye. It was assumed that she insisted on her own bedroom almost from the start of their marriage, and when describing Daphne, Alan's niece declared: 'She was anti-sex'. Many years later Alan would write: 'The doom of Holy Matrimony is the separate room'.

Daphne's wealthy family employed several servants, and when she left home to marry Alan, she was joined by her personal maid Gertrude and a cook called Mrs Penn who stayed with them for years. To Daphne, appearances, style and elegance were more important than spontaneous declarations of romantic love, but the couple were always closely bonded by their shared sense of humour. She would dutifully listen to her husband talk about cricket for hours, although when she heard applause during a match at Lord's once, she was overheard to remark: 'Another goal I suppose?'

In those early days of matrimony, Alan still dreamt of rising through the ranks to become the editor of *Punch*, and when the editor Owen Seaman was knighted and looked set to move on to greater things, Daphne did all she could to encourage her husband's glittering career. He also became a regular contributor to *Sphere* magazine, his work was receiving glowing praise and his reputation was soaring sky high as one of London's great wits. One review said: 'Scores of young writers tried to imitate him,' while the *Times Literary Supplement* said Alan had 'one of the most engaging silly senses of humour in the world'.

He was confident that a bright future lay ahead, and Alan would later look back on those pre-war years as the happiest of his life. But all that was to drastically change in 1914, when their newly wedded bliss was shattered by the outbreak of the First World War, and Alan found himself forced to join up and spend four long and gruelling years in the army. He would never fully recover from the horrors and inhumanity he endured on the battlefields of the Somme, which left him a changed man. The memories haunted him forever: 'It makes me almost physically sick to think of that nightmare of mental and moral degradation, the war,' he said afterwards. 'War is the most babyish and laughably idiotic thing that this poor world has evolved.'

He never supported the conflict but his pacifist views put him in the minority, as it was considered unpatriotic and cowardly not to want to fight for your country at the time. But the atmosphere in London quickly became intolerable for men who did not immediately volunteer to join up, *Punch* was full of jokes about 'shirkers' and, by February 1915, Alan had no choice but to enlist. He reported for duty, serving as an officer in the Fourth Battalion of the Royal Warwickshire Regiment. He hated the loss of freedom during his training sessions in the Isle of Wight and Weymouth but at least he could still write and was in daily contact with Daphne. The death toll was heavy, and as news of the casualties filtered through from the frontline, he knew he was lucky to be alive.

Almost a century later, in April 2013, startling revelations emerged that Alan had in fact been secretly working as a propaganda writer for a mysterious intelligence unit, known only as MI7b. Although the unit's entire archive was thought to have been destroyed years earlier, a stash of documents saved from a skip revealed Alan's clandestine role, along with a never-before seen satirical poem imagining what great writers like Shakespeare and Tennyson would have written had they too been working as propagandists. These last remaining classified documents only survived because a member of the unit,

Captain James Lloyd, had taken them home and kept them hidden until his great nephew Jeremy Arter came to clear out his house following his death, and discovered them concealed in a trunk. The papers are the only surviving evidence of MI7's existence, and Mr Arter who also worked in army propaganda in the Royal Army Educational Corps, explained:

> *Much of the household belongings were due to go in a skip. I was about to throw everything away but, leafing through, I saw a book with MI7b written on it and decided to take a closer look. When I turned the front cover and I saw the name A.A. Milne I knew it would be a historic document.*

MI7b was established in 1916 to sustain support for the war when soldiers were being killed in their thousands, and anti-war movements were sweeping war-torn Europe. Alan was among around twenty writers who were selected from the cream of British talent to produce more than 7,500 positive newspaper articles about Victoria Cross winners, heroism, and sanitised accounts of life in the trenches between 1916 and 1918. But the work sat uncomfortably with Alan, who objected strongly to the conflict. Mr Arter added:

> *There are about 150 separate articles made up of pencil drafts, manuscripts, and typescripts, along with notebooks and photographs. I was astonished when my research showed that they were meant to have been destroyed soon after the war because they were deemed "too incriminating". He broke every rule in the book and took his work home with him – that's the only reason any evidence survived.*

According to intelligence historian Andrew Cook, the unit worked closely with newspaper publishers and kept an eye on the foreign press, countered negative stories, and wrote material intended for leaflets dropped by hot air balloons:

> *It was set up in 1916 when casualties were mounting and there*

were large numbers of dead. This was having a major impact.
As the war soldiered on into 1916 and 1917 there was
unofficial industrial action that concerned the government.
Prime Minister Lloyd George and his government also knew
that the Russian revolution started in a small way after food
shortages and there were fears that could happen here.

To distract himself from the horrors he saw at every turn, Alan started work on a play, which has not survived, but became the idea for his first children's book *Once On A Time*. 'This book was written in 1915,' he explained in the preface. 'For the amusement of my wife and myself at a time when life was not very amusing.' He also found time, in his spare hours between instructing soldiers and composing propaganda for the government, to write a three-act play called *Wurzel-Flummery*, a comedy revolving around the unlikely question of whether anyone would be willing to assume the ridiculous name of Wurzel-Flummery in order to receive an inheritance of £50,000. Alan was given a day's leave to be taken to lunch at the Carlton Grill in London by the actor Dennis Eadie who was keen to star in the play. Afterwards he and Daphne returned to the Isle of Wight together, to a rented cottage in Sandown; thirty minutes after they had gone to bed that evening, there was a loud knocking at the front door. It was the news they had dreaded: Alan's battalion was being shipped out, and forty-eight hours later he was in France.

He knew he had been lucky so far, working in signals and communication, which kept him far from the bullets and bombs. But when he arrived at Bully-Grenay in France, he wrote heart-wrenching letters to Ken and H.G. Wells describing his disgust at not just the disease, filth and fear he witnessed in the trenches, but also the sheer meaningless lunacy of the entire war: 'I simply can't tell you how I loathe the Army,' he said. 'This is a beastly war.'

Daphne could not bear to be alone, so went to stay with her mother at Burnham-on-Crouch, not far from the barracks at Colchester where she was able to receive comforting news about Alan. After five months in France, Alan was struck down by trench fever and sent back to a military hospital in Oxford, where he woke after several fitful days to find Daphne crying at the end of his bed. In the harsh November days following Alan's return home, the Somme became a bloodbath, with the Allied forces suffering the loss of hundreds of thousands of lives in some of the worst atrocities of the war. Later known as The Big Push, it would almost certainly have claimed his life. Alan could not quite believe how fortunate he had been to escape the battlefield when he did, and while it would be many months before his health fully recovered, he never forgot what he had seen. He re-joined his regiment on the Isle of Wight and continued working as a signals instructor while editing the script of *Wurzel-Flummery* for the London production, which opened in April 1917. But his health was still frail and the long hours took their toll, so he was sent to convalesce at Queen Victoria's former country home Osborne House, arriving at the same time as war poet Robert Graves who found his fellow writer 'in his least humorous vein'.

By the end of the year however, Alan had made a full recovery and landed himself a desk job in the War Office in London, which freed up plenty of time to work on his latest play *Belinda*. When it opened, starring Irene Vanbrugh, he was astonished to find himself being compared to the writers he had long admired including George Bernard Shaw and Oscar Wilde. But it did not feel right to celebrate since the German forces had renewed their offensive and London was suffering badly from night after night of deadly air raids. In just three weeks the Allies lost 400,000 more men and the theatres all went dark: 'It was difficult to regard its ill-fortune as a matter of much importance,' Alan said.

While the plays and the Army were boosting his income a little, he was not yet earning enough to stop sending contributions to *Punch*, and planned to return to the magazine office as soon as the war was over. Peace was declared in November 1918 and although many jobs had been held open for soldiers, Sir Owen made it clear they had not really expected Alan to return to work full time. Daphne was devastated when he broke the news that he would never make it to the editor's chair:

CHAPTER THREE

I promised her that we shouldn't starve, he said. I promised to make a success of the theatre. It was a little like telling a woman whose loved cottage has been burnt down that you will build a more expensive one in the ruins. It doesn't really comfort her at the time.

He also wrote to H.G. Wells: 'I have retired from *Punch*…it is rather like ceasing to be a member of the Church of England'. The army received Alan's official resignation letter in February 1919, meaning he and Daphne were at last free to return to their apartment overlooking the Thames, where Alan could concentrate on his plays and the young couple could enjoy their social life in London again. On 7 March 1919, Alan's friend E.V. Lucas proposed him as a member of the exclusive Garrick Club, a private gentleman's club in Covent Garden, describing his occupation as 'author, journalist, dramatist'. Alan was able to mingle and network with a host of interesting actors and writers. Over the years he made some extremely useful connections, and became so fond of the place that he rewarded the club with a huge share of the *Pooh* royalties on his death, and a valuable archive of his letters still remains in the oak-panelled club library today.

Reflecting the strong national appetite for comedy in the aftermath of the war years, his first real success was a farce called *Mr Pim Passes By*, which he wrote with actress Lillah McCarthy in mind as his leading lady. He judged accurately that theatregoers were not looking for anything too serious and, following rave reviews and 246 performances in London, it also opened for a successful run in New York. *Mr Pim* would continue to be staged on and off for years, earning Alan vast sums in royalties for the rest of his life. It also meant his name was becoming better known on the other side of the Atlantic, and before long his plays were up and running in numerous theatres around the United States, as well as at home in Britain.

Next, Alan began work on a detective novel, *The Red House Mystery*, which he dedicated to his father saying: 'Like all really nice people, you have a weakness for detective stories and feel that there are not enough of them. So, after all that you have done for me, the least that I can do for you is to write you one'.

It was swiftly followed by a particularly productive period, as plays seemed to flow freely from his pen, including *The Red Feathers* and *The Great Broxopp* as well as four screenplays for Minerva Films. It was the early days of cinema, and as talking films were becoming increasingly popular, many writers wanted to hop on the screenwriting bandwagon. But Alan was not keen; he found the slow pace of the film making process frustrating. He had never been one to suffer fools, and in his opinion the new world of movie making appeared to be full of them: 'God how slowly their minds moved! Other people's minds. What were their brains doing all that time? They had to say things over and over again to themselves before any meaning emerged. How hellish to be born with a brain like that!'

Alan, on the other hand, worked very fast, and a flurry of new theatre scripts soon appeared including *The Lucky One, Give Me Yesterday, Ariadne, To Have The Honour, Portrait of a Gentleman in Slippers, Miss Marlow At Play*, and *The Fourth Wall*, also known as *The Perfect Alibi*. But while work was going better than ever, there were problems at home as the Milnes were both becoming increasingly worried about Daphne's failure to conceive – they had been married for almost six years, and were eager to start a family. They tried to ease up on their hectic social schedule, preferring to spend as many weekends as they could at Daphne's father's house in Hampshire, although their tranquillity was often shattered by fierce arguments with her brother Aubrey who was known as the black sheep of the family and would repeatedly ask Alan to loan him money: 'The requests got larger and the repayments slower until the latter ceased but the former continued,' he said. Gradually the rift between them deepened until Alan and Daphne stopped communicating with him altogether.

At last, in the spring of 1920, came the eagerly anticipated announcement that Daphne was pregnant, and they moved to a larger house in Mallord Street SW3 to prepare for the arrival of their first and only son. Christopher Robin Milne was born at home on 21 August 1920, weighing in at a healthy 10lbs with a head of thick brown curly hair, but it was a long and traumatic birth, on a particularly hot summer's day, from which Daphne never fully recovered. Alan said afterwards: 'To me, the miracle of human birth is more worthy of awe than the miracle of virgin birth. What a piece of work is a man!'

They had originally intended to call the baby William and so from day one Christopher Robin was affectionately known by his parents as Billy, and later as Billy Moon – from his own pronunciation of Milne. Alan initially seemed somewhat disappointed in the new arrival, and later wrote to a friend confessing that he had been hoping for a daughter: 'We did rather want a Rosemary, but I expect we shall be just as happy with this gentleman'. And he later wrote in his autobiography:

I am not inordinately fond of or interested in children; their appeal to me is a physical appeal such as the young of other animals make. I have never felt in the least sentimental about them, or no more sentimental than one becomes for a moment over a puppy or a kitten.

Christopher himself confirmed the idea that Alan was uneasy around young children by writing in his own memoir:

Some people are good with children. Others are not. It is a gift. You either have it or you don't. My father didn't. Later on it was different, very different. But I am thinking of nursery days. He added: *If I cannot say that I loved my parents, it is only because in those early days, I just didn't know them well enough.*

Christopher occupied the nursery up on the top floor of the house, where he would sleep and eat with his nanny, and was allowed to visit his parents after their meals: 'My occasional encounters with my parents stand out as the events of the day,' he wrote. 'I would play 'boofy games' with my mother, getting more and more excited until the arrival of Nanny would bring it all to an end and I would be swept upstairs to my bath.'

Christopher may not have actually been called Rosemary, but he was often dressed as a girl, had long hair 'at a time when boys didn't have long hair' and his best friend was a little girl called Anne Darlington, who was 8 months older and lived just half a mile away in Beaufort Mansions. Since neither of them had brothers or sisters they forged a strong bond that kept them close for the rest of their lives. Anne often joined the Milnes on family outings and holidays, and their friendship inspired many of Alan's most popular poems including:

> *Where is Anne?*

> *Head above the buttercups,*
> *Walking by the stream,*
> *Down among the buttercups.*

And:

> *'When Anne and I go out a walk,*
> *We hold each other's hand and talk*
> *Of all the things we mean to do*
> *When Anne and I are forty-two.*

After Christopher was born, Alan and Daphne continued to travel extensively, even spending a month in Italy when he was a baby, so much of his care was left to their nanny Olive Rand, who continued working for the family for the next nine years, until Christopher left for boarding school. Describing his parent's detached attitude, Christopher said: 'If I wasn't a full-time job, I was at least a part time hobby'. But he adored Olive, who he nicknamed Nou, and said:

> *I was all hers and remained all hers until the age of nine. So much were we together that Nanny became almost a part of me. Other people hovered around the edges, but they meant little. My total loyalty was to her. I might not have missed my mother, and would certainly not have missed my father, I would have missed Nanny most desolately.*

CHAPTER THREE

When she did eventually leave in 1930, he finally transferred his affections to Alan:

I was still as shy as ever; worse, if anything. I still needed someone to cling to. So I clung to my father, said Christopher. *For nearly ten more years I was to cling to him, adoring him as I had adored Nanny, so that he too became almost a part of me, at first, no doubt, to his delight, later perhaps to his anxiety.*

Years later, after she had retired, Olive suggested in an interview with the *Sunday Times* that perhaps Christopher's memory had played tricks on him over the years and to the best of her recollection, Alan had never ignored or scorned him when he was small: 'Mr Milne always entered into the spirit of things,' she said, 'and spoke to the toys as if they were real people'.

Despite their somewhat conflicting recollections of his early childhood, Christopher always insisted that he was not the same boy that his father wrote about:

The Christopher Robin who appears in so many of the poems is not always me, he said. *For this was where my name, so totally useless to me personally, came into its own: it was a wonderful name for writing poetry round. Sometimes my father is using it to described something I did, and sometimes he is borrowing it to describe something he did as a child, and sometimes he is using it to describe something that any child might have done.*

Alan maintained that the poems and stories were all about his son, but as Christopher was often at pains to point out, the boy in the stories was nothing more than a work of fiction, and that Alan tended to draw upon his own childhood adventures with Ken for inspiration:

There was one great difference between my father and myself when we were children, Christopher said. *He had an elder brother; I had not. So he was never alone in the dark. Lying in bed with the lights out he could so easily be "talking to a dragon; and feeling brave", knowing that if the dragon turned fierce he had only to reach out a hand and there would be Ken in the next bed. But I could take no such risks. I had to keep reminding myself that the dragon was a bedtime story, not a real one.*

I continued to have night fears for a long time. When, later, I went to boarding school, this was my one consolation when the holidays came to an end: there were no dragons in dormitories.

Alan clearly tried his best to create a happy childhood for his son, and once even arranged for an actor called Louis Goodrich, who he had met at The Garrick Club, to dress up in full military uniform to surprise Christopher. At the time Christopher was fascinated by soldiers, but later suggested that Alan may have regretted introducing him to Louis as they struck up an unlikely friendship:

It was difficult for him, of course, Christopher said. For there was Nanny always in the way. Nanny who claimed so much of my affection. And on the rare occasions when Nanny was out of the room, there was my mother in her place. Where did he fit in? Nowhere special.

And now here was Soldier. You could see how my eyes lit up at the very thought of Soldier, at the mere mention of his name. You could see (or you could be told) how he made me laugh, how I adored him.

No, my father couldn't compete. Did this make him, I wonder, a little jealous, a little sad? Did he secretly envy those who had the gift? My poor father! All that was left to him were family visits to the London Zoo or family walks through the Sussex woods, and perhaps a few brief minutes of good-night story.

CHAPTER FOUR

'The cold's so cold, and the hot's so hot.
Oh! God bless Daddy - I quite forgot.'

While Christopher Robin was still a baby, Alan found the time to finish two plays *The Truth About Blayds* and *The Dover Road*, which became staples of amateur dramatic societies and repertory companies around the world and meant the Milnes were becoming very well off financially. In January 1922 his father John was able to boast: 'Alan has at this moment five plays running! Three in America, one in London, one in Liverpool'.

With his reputation as a successful playwright now firmly established, Alan could start to enjoy the fruits of his labours, and most days he would have lunch at The Garrick Club: 'Mrs Milne encourages me to go to my club every day; she says it brightens me up and that I bring her back plenty of good stories,' he said in an interview.

With Alan out at the club, Daphne had a chance to see her friends and with their ten-year anniversary approaching, the couple were spending more and more time apart, as there were very few things that they really enjoyed doing together. Alan avoided professional football, all blood sports, racing and gambling. He also disliked music, preferring to spend as much spare time as he could on the golf course. Although Daphne had taken lessons when they first got together, they had both long since given up any hope of her ever becoming a keen golfer. She preferred browsing London department stores such as Harrods and Harvey Nichols, and constantly hired decorators to change the appearance of rooms in their house – although Alan complained about the noise and upheaval, and he loathed the smell of paint. Daphne was always immaculately turned out and was a frequent visitor to the Elizabeth Arden beauty spa. She became well known for following the latest fashions, and her vast collection of hats – she even had her own personal milliner.

Alan, meanwhile, was in the mood for a break from writing plays. He changed tack one evening after catching a glimpse of Billy, who was then aged 2, kneeling by his cot and saying his prayers. Their nanny Olive recalled Alan watching his son closely, and then disappearing off to his study: 'Then I heard him going away down the stairs chuckling as if he was very pleased about something,' she said. Although he had no time for Christianity, and found the sight of a child praying to be overly sentimental, Alan jotted down a sweet short poem for Daphne, and called it *Vespers*. He told his wife that if she could get it published then she could keep the money; Daphne relished the challenge, and *Vespers* appeared in *Vanity Fair* magazine in January 1923. She initially received just $50, but over the years royalties for *Vespers* flooded in to the tune of many millions of pounds, and it turned out to be by far the most generous present Alan had ever given his wife.

The family was enjoying more and more weekends escaping the bustle of London life and visiting friends in the countryside, so it made sense to consider buying a place of their own. The author Kenneth Graham offered to sell them his Berkshire home, which he was leaving in the anguished aftermath of his son's death on a nearby railway line. Alan did not buy the property, but the two writers struck up a friendship and stayed in contact for many years, with Alan readily agreeing to dramatise Graham's hugely successful children's book *The Wind In The Willows*. His play, which he called *Toad of Toad Hall*, did not make it on to the stage until several years later but Alan was thrilled to be asked to write the adaptation: 'I shall love doing it,' he wrote to Graham's publisher. 'In fact, as soon as I got your letter, I began sketching it out. It's no use talking to me about novels now – I'm much too excited about this here play.'

Until that point, Alan had always made a point of avoiding writing for children, because he feared it would not be taken seriously: 'No one can write a book which children will like, unless he writes it for himself first,' Alan said. But *Toad* sparked something new in Alan, and during a rainy family holiday to Wales he found himself composing several verses for children: 'It is not the work of a poet becoming playful, nor of a lover of children expressing his love, nor of a prose-writer knocking together a few jingles for the little ones, it is the work of a light-verse writer taking his job seriously, even though he is taking it into the nursery,' Alan explained.

Returning to London, he broke the unexpected news that his next book was to be a collection of children's verse. E.V. Lucas, his publisher at Methuen, was shocked and suggested that perhaps Alan was just bored, and his daily life needed more structure. He even advised Alan to return to *Punch* for the sake of his literary career which he presumed to be in free-fall, but with money flowing in from productions of his plays around Europe and America, he did not really need to work all that hard, and was ready to try something new: 'I think my indolence is more apparent than real or perhaps I should say that it is real, but I overcome it pretty well. Quite frankly I could not bear to write regularly for *Punch* again. It would make me miserable,' he told Lucas.

As soon as Lucas saw the poems, he had no doubt they would make an excellent book, but knew it was crucial to find the right illustrator. And so, when Lucas next happened to find himself at the *Punch* table sitting next to one of the magazine's best cartoonists Ernest Shepard, he suggested seeing what Alan thought of his drawings. Alan already knew Shepard's work very well, although the two men had little in common and were never friends. They had completely different attitudes and temperaments, and clashed over their attitudes to war – Alan was a pacifist while Shepard was always fascinated by guns. Shepard described Alan as 'a rather cagey man', but the writer was absolutely delighted by the first illustrations he was shown, for the poem *Puppy and I*.

Methuen knew they had a hit on their hands, but Alan's joy was tarnished by grave worries about Ken's rapidly declining health. His brother had been diagnosed with tuberculosis, and in the spring of 1924 he was advised to resign from the Ministry of Pensions and move from Croydon to the fresh air of the Somerset countryside. When Alan heard about Ken leaving the Civil Service at the age of 43 he invited him to lunch at the National Liberal Club and offered his complete financial support to the family. With four children still in full-time education it would have been impossible for them to manage on Ken's pension; so Alan happily agreed to pay all the school fees and medical bills. It came as a huge relief to Ken, who had no choice but to accept. And from that day until his last, Alan wrote long letters to Ken in an attempt to cheer and entertain him. He visited Somerset several times too, although Daphne never went with him, and Christopher could not remember meeting his uncle.

That summer Alan and Daphne finally found the perfect country retreat they had been searching for, Cotchford Farm, in the quaint Sussex village of Hartfield, on the edge of Ashdown Forest. To meet Daphne's exacting standards, renovations on the property took months, but Alan was immediately enchanted by the stunning scenery that surrounded the farm, which became the inspiration for the Hundred Acre Wood, where *Winnie-the-Pooh* would soon take up residence under the name of Sanders. They all fell in love with the place, although Christopher had been surprised that his father wanted to leave town:

He was a Londoner, a real Londoner with a deep love of London in his bones. For him the country had always been not where you lived, but where you went. Where you went on holiday. Where you went to do something – to ride a bicycle, to climb a hill, to look for birds' nests, to play golf. Like a dog, he couldn't just be in the country, sitting or strolling aimlessly. It had to be a proper walk, a walk with a purpose, planned beforehand, worked out on the map even. And you couldn't go alone, you had to be with somebody, with me perhaps, or with the whole family, Nanny included. Like a dog, too, he was happiest of all when chasing a ball.

But from then on the Milnes spent every weekend and holiday in Sussex, Alan loved the peace and tranquillity, as well as watching Christopher roaming the picturesque countryside and having adventures with the new friends he made. A little girl who lived locally inspired the character of Pooh's timid and faithful friend Piglet, and many years later, when she was 92 years old, Veronica Rushworth-Lund recalled fond and vivid memories of days spent with the family at Cotchford, where Alan was the first to nickname her Piglet: 'I was the smallest and youngest of a group of children that knew Christopher Robin and played with him,' she explained. 'I was always the littlest ... and I was rather pink at the time.' Piglet, who 'lived in a very grand house in the middle of beech tree', always wore a green knitted jumper that reached all the way down to his knees. He was afraid of 'Heffalumps' but was brave and resourceful when adventure called.

Veronica went on:

There was a field and stream where the 'Poohsticks Bridge' was. We used to see how many times we could cross it on branches without getting our feet wet. We usually got fairly muddy. And, of course, we played Poohsticks and Clock Golf, too – where putts are taken at the hole from different points on a circle around it – on a lawn which sloped and the ball always ran into the stream.

Christopher Robin loved the garden and the field. He was like any other little boy. He wasn't particularly precious,

Veronica was a tomboy who would borrow Christopher's shorts to avoid getting her dress muddy during their games. Cleaning up after their long games usually fell to Olive, who Veronica also recalled with great fondness, adding that Christopher's nanny provided Alan with the inspiration for Kanga, the doting mother of Roo: 'She was just very like the character of Kanga,' Veronica said, mimicking Olive's affectionate voice: '"Come on, dear, it's time for bed". She was very nice and a very efficient nurse. Everybody seems old to children, but she was about 35.' In the stories Piglet was once given a bath by Kanga and protested loudly about being scrubbed with a large lathery flannel. Veronica admitted she was exactly the same when Olive attempted to wash her with a soapy flannel too.

Veronica also revealed childhood memories of Daphne, who as a girl had gone to school with her mother. And she remembered Alan as: 'A very nice, good-looking man, with an elegant and amusing wife', describing them as a very glamorous couple who were 'the Beckhams of their day'. Alan was a busy man, but would make sure he took time away from his desk to play with the children when he was down from London: 'He liked playing if we were there for the weekend, he would be with us. He wouldn't be writing,' she added.

Veronica and Christopher also went to a local nursery school together, beginning a friendship that would last into adulthood. As her own brother was six years older than her and already away at boarding school, she felt particularly close to Christopher, who became a sort of surrogate sibling. She had only happy memories of their shared childhood, and never witnessed the cruel bullying and taunts that Christopher later endured at boarding school: 'He was a quite ordinary, happy child,' she said of his early years. 'It wasn't until later that he got rather ragged about his father's poems and became self-conscious.'

Back then Christopher would happily enter into the spirit of things. In 1929, he and Veronica took part in a parade of children dressed as characters from the *Pooh* books, part of a pageant at Ashdown Forest. Alan had asked the children to wear costumes, and Veronica cheerfully appeared as Piglet. There were no signs then of the problems and resentment that was to come: 'I quite liked being Christopher Robin and being famous,' he recalled. 'There were indeed times – as at pageants – when it was exciting and made me feel grand and important. But of the ripples of fame that came through my nursery door, each was judged firmly on its merits.'

Veronica also vividly recalled acting out a scene in which she had to deliver a red balloon to gloomy Eeyore for his birthday: 'If you know the E.H. Shepard drawings from the books well, you know that Piglet falls and bursts the balloon,' she said. 'That was the high point of the play. The balloon had to burst, and I had to carry a pin to make sure it did. Falling on a red balloon sticks in your memory.' Christopher willingly played himself. Veronica still has a prized copy of *Winnie-the-Pooh* which she was given as a wedding present by

CHAPTER FOUR

Alan, dedicated to: 'The one and only never to be forgotten Piglet, with love from A.A. Milne.'

As soon as Shepard's drawings were finished in 1924, *When We Were Very Young* hit the shelves, but nobody was prepared for its success. Within just eight weeks it had become a best seller in both the UK and America. Bookshops requested thousands more copies every day, and the printers could hardly keep pace with the enormous demand. Alan dedicated the book 'To the little boy who calls himself Billy Moon', and readers were immediately entranced by the boy and the whimsical verses, which included *Buckingham Palace, Halfway Down* and *Three Little Foxes*. Critics raved about the poems, which featured sweet children who used words like 'cos' and 'nuffin' and 'purfickly'. Nannies and nurseries appeared in several of the forty-five poems, and the charming period illustrations enhanced their popularity hugely. Alan's own childhood memories played an important part in these poems, particularly when he described children escaping for adventures away from the constraints of their parents or nannies. But there were also hidden menaces and uncertainties – such as the bears waiting to eat the sillies who tread on the lines of the street, or the Brownies lurking behind the curtains. There were constant worries of beetles, mice, or mothers going missing but the children, while highly imaginative, tended to be endearingly well-behaved and polite.

Alan was astounded by the popularity of his poetry in the United States, where to his amazement *When We Were Very Young* was reprinted twenty-three times within the first year. He received scores of glowing reviews and effusive letters of appreciation from thirty-eight state governors, six members of the Cabinet, three Justices of the Supreme Court, eleven Rear Admirals, twelve Major Generals, Fred Astaire, and even President Coolidge declared himself a fan. The poems sparked popular catchphrases, and people no longer asked for simply butter, but for 'some butter for the Royal slice of bread'. They had been aimed at children but appealed to people of all ages, from every corner of the globe. Flattered at being likened to his literary heroes including Lewis Carroll and Rudyard Kipling, Alan had to accept that life would never be the same again. He began to move in the highest social circles – he was even invited to dine with Princess Marie Louise, granddaughter of Queen Victoria, but admitted afterwards: 'I said 'Ma'am' as little as possible, put my foot in it once or twice probably, withdrew it with a loud sucking noise and continued cheerfully'.

But in the midst of all the widespread acclaim, the contrasts between his good fortune and Ken's sad situation were stark. As his health failed further, Ken tried to reply to as many of Alan's cheerful letters as he could, knowing it was too late for him to ever be free from his younger brother's long shadow. When Alan heard news of ground-breaking medical treatment in Denmark he urged Ken to take him up on his offer to pay for an eight-week trip across the North Sea to meet Danish doctors, but Ken did not have the strength to travel.

Meanwhile a blindingly bright spotlight was beginning to shine on the small boy at the centre of all the furore. Christopher Robin was suddenly very, very famous, and other children found it easy to poke fun at him. It did not help that one of the first photographs circulated in various newspapers of the author and his blonde, curly-haired child was captioned 'A.A. Milne, his wife and little daughter'.

At first the being in the public eye seemed quite natural to Christopher Robin, who could not really remember a time before being asked to sign his autograph on copies of the book, from the age of three or four. Daphne suggested it was no more unusual than other children finding their pictures in family photo albums, and initially Christopher did not seem troubled by the attention that came from his starring role.

Their sanctuary was Cotchford, where Alan and Christopher developed a shared passion for the game of cricket: 'His is taking after me,' he told a journalist visiting the house. 'I was a mathematician and a cricketer when I was his age! I don't know that I would specially want him to write.'

While sales of *When We Were Very Young* flourished way beyond all expectations, Daphne enjoyed working as Alan's unofficial secretary, but when they were in the countryside she preferred to be left to her own devices, happily absorbed in planting flowers in the garden. She became so passionate about it that Alan nicknamed her Daffodil. When he wanted to escape, Alan could be found on the golf course, watching rugby at Twickenham, or cheering on his alma mater in the annual Oxford versus Cambridge boat race. He and Christopher spent hours practicing on the make-shift cricket pitch Alan had specially built for them in the meadow at Cotchford, listening to Test Matches on the wireless, or travelling to London to watch games at the Oval cricket ground. Alan would always take the same picnic of ham sandwiches, egg sandwiches, and a paper bag of cherries for them to share. But looking back on those days, Christopher said the relationship between them was already far from perfect:

So there I was, very close indeed to my father, adoring him, admiring him, accepting his ideas, yet at the same time immensely sensitive, easily wounded, quick to take offence. An accidental word of reproof or criticism from him and tears would stream from my eyes and a barrier of silence would descend between us keeping us apart for days. So he had to be careful what he said. But provided he was careful, I was, I imagine, an easy child to teach. His knowledge, his opinions, his beliefs could be passed on to me and I would eagerly accept them as my own. It was too easy, almost. In fact it was dangerously easy.

When asked to describe his family, as he often was, Christopher said:

Mr Milne. An odd mixture of opposites: shy, yet at the same time self-confident; modest, yet proud of what he had done; quiet, yet a good talker; warm, yet with a thin lip and an ice-cold eye that might, if you said the wrong thing, be pretty chilling; sympathetic, yet unsympathetic to what he felt was stupidity; friendly, yet picking his friends with care. Next, Mrs Milne. A certain hot and cold about her too. You had to say the right thing. Obviously very proud of her husband and wrapped up in his work, though perhaps even more wrapped up in her garden.

It was clear to everybody that Alan and Daphne were vastly different in their interests and their temperaments, but their marriage appeared solid and they were apparently happy enough to let each other have their separate hobbies. Christopher watched his parents closely, and years later he observed:

While my mother dug, my father putted. Does this sound like ant and grasshopper? In a way it was. But you can look at it another way. To each his trade. My father was a writer: this was his work. All he wanted from my mother was her encouragement and praise. My mother was a gardener, and praised and encouragement was all she wished for in return.

The garden for my father was mainly where you putted and where you admired my mother's labours. It was also where, after lunch, you sought out a sheltered spot, and, armed with deckchair, cushions, rugs and pullovers, retired there to reverberate gently until teatime.

CHAPTER FIVE

'We will be friends until forever, just you wait and see.'

While Alan wrote, Daphne always spent a great deal of her time shopping; indeed she was the one who had bought Christopher Robin a teddy bear from the exclusive London department store *Harrods* for his first birthday. The toy, whom they decided to call Edward Bear, immediately became his constant companion, travelling with the family up and down to Sussex every weekend, driven by their chauffeur Burnside – who had attempted to teach Alan how to drive, but he always hated doing it. And it was during those long car journeys that Christopher and his mother began to make up voices for Edward Bear: 'He and his mother gave them life,' Alan said. Daphne later claimed it was not her but their son and his bear who did the talking: 'They indulged in lengthy conversations,' she said. 'Christopher interpolating fierce growls for the bear, feeling thoroughly convinced about it.' Edward made his first of many appearances in the poem

Teddy Bear:

He gets what exercise he can
By falling off the ottoman,
But generally seems to lack
The energy to clamber back.

Christopher and Edward were inseparable, and over time he also became the proud owner of a gloomy toy donkey called Eeyore, which was a present for Christmas in 1921, and a stuffed Piglet thanks to a neighbour in Chelsea. There have been many differing explanations over the intervening years of how Christopher's beloved bear later came to be called Winnie-the-Pooh, but the most likely is that he was named after an American black bear called Winnie who was one of the most popular animals at London Zoo, and certainly Christopher's favourite on the frequent visits he made with his parents and nanny. During the First World War, when she was a small cub, the bear was smuggled across the Atlantic by Canadian Lieutenant Harry Colebourn. A trained vet, Colebourn was on his way to Europe when he saw the young bear for sale in White River, Ontario, and bought her for just £12 from a hunter who had killed the creature's mother. He named her Winnipeg after his home city in Manitoba, Canada, and it was soon shortened to Winnie. Winnie became the unofficial mascot of his army regiment, the Princess Pat's, who trained on Salisbury Plain in Wiltshire. After Colebourn was sent to fight in France in 1914, the bear was left in the safekeeping of the Royal Zoological Society, and she remained at London Zoo until she died of old age in May 1934. A statue of Colebourn and his bear now stands in Assiniboine Park in Winnipeg, and there is still a sculpture of her in the zoo today.

Children, including Christopher Robin, were allowed to feed Winnie but new research came to light in 2015 revealing that the skull of the bear showed signs of tooth decay because she had eaten far too much honey. Curators recently studied the skull, which has been kept at the Royal College of Surgeons since the 1930s, and their close examinations showed that Winnie suffered from various significant dental problems including chronic periodontitis, an inflammation, and loss of connective tissues supporting the teeth. The skull has been put on display at the Hunterian Museum so visitors can learn all about the real life Pooh. Director of Museums and Archives at the Royal College of Surgeons Sam Alberti said: '*Winnie-the-Pooh* remains one of the most popular children's stories ever since Pooh Bear was brought to life on the pages of A.A. Milne's books in 1926.

Children and adults who visit the Hunterian Museum will now have an opportunity to learn about the real Winnie and how she inspired A.A. Milne. Her story and presence in our collection are

a reminder of how learning about animal health can enhance
our understanding and care for species around the world.

The children's author Enid Blyton once claimed that Christopher had actually played with the real bear, and there are old pictures showing Christopher inside the enclosure feeding Winnie honey from a spoon: 'The bear hugged Christopher Robin and they had a glorious time together, rolling about and pulling ears and all sorts of things,' Blyton wrote.

That explains the Winnie part of the character's name, but there is also some confusion over the where 'Pooh' came from. Daphne would tell people that her son exclaimed 'Oh Pooh!' on meeting the bear at the zoo, because of the smell coming from Winnie's cage. But Alan insisted that the name came about during one of the Milne family's visits to a holiday cottage called The Decoy, near Arundel in Sussex, where Christopher Robin fed a swan on the lake and decided to call him Pooh: 'This is a very fine name for a swan,' he told his father. 'Because if you call him and he doesn't come then you can pretend that you were just saying 'Pooh' to show how little you wanted him. 'We took the name with us, as we didn't think the swan would want it anymore.' In response to hundreds of questions surrounding the mystery of Winnie-the-Pooh's gender, Alan wrote:

> *When I first heard his name, I said, just as you are going to say,*
> *"But I thought he was a boy?"*
> *"So did I," said Christopher Robin.*
> *"Then you can't call him Winnie?"*
> *"I don't."*
> *"But you said –"*
> *"He's Winnie-ther-Pooh. Don't you know what 'ther' means?"*
> *"Ah yes, now I do," I said quickly; and I hope you do too, because*
> *it's all the explanation you're going to get.*

Alan had not tackled prose for children until December 1925 when he was given the task of coming up with a story for a special Christmas

Eve edition of the *Evening News*, and as he racked his brains for a suitable idea, Daphne suggested using one of the bedtime stories he told Christopher. And so he began:

> *This is Big Bear, coming downstairs now, bump-bump on the back of his head, behind Christopher Robin. It is, as far as he knows, the only way of coming downstairs, but sometimes he feels that there really is another way, if only he could stop bumping for a moment and think of it.*

That now famous paragraph became be the introduction to *Winnie-the-Pooh*, and in the New Year he started work on his first collection of short stories for children, with the toys in Christopher's nursery at the heart of it. He invented Owl and Rabbit, and then he and Daphne returned to the toy department at *Harrods* on a mission to acquire new characters. There they found Kanga, Roo, and Tigger:

> *Both Kanga and Tigger were later arrivals,* Christopher said. *Presents for my parents, carefully chosen, not just for the delights they might give to their new owner, but also for their literary possibilities. So there they were, and to a certain extent their characters were theirs from birth. As my father said, making it all sound very simple, you only had to look at them to see at once that Eeyore was gloomy, Piglet squeaky, Tigger bouncy, and so on. But of course there was much more to it than that.*

Alan knew the value of Shepard's drawings, and asked him to illustrate new editions of *Once On A Time* and his old children's play *Make Believe*, but he found himself in great demand and did not have the time. Known as Kipper to his friends, Shepard did however agree to work on the layout of Alan's new book of stories, although theirs was never a particularly easy partnership: 'I always had to start again at the beginning with Milne every time I met him, I think he retired into himself – very often and for long periods,' Shepard said.

Alan invited him to see Christopher's toys for himself, but Shepard felt there was no need since he had been drawing bears for years, based on his own son Graham's teddy called Growler. And it is in fact Growler who would soon become so familiar to millions, made famous by Shepard's distinctive pencil drawings. The only photograph in the world of the toy bear was uncovered in a family archive in 2015. The grainy sepia picture, believed to have been taken around 1913 when Graham was 6 years old, shows him with his sister Mary standing next to Growler. The photo was discovered by researchers who were trawling through the vast archives of The Shepard Trust, custodians of all Shepard's work, and experts now believe that the incredible find is the only known picture of Growler in existence. It has since been published in a book called *Shepard's War*, which tells the story of the artist's time on the frontline during the First World War. Growler himself was passed down to Graham's daughter Minette Hunt, but sadly has not survived.

Author James Campbell, a trustee of the Shepard Trust and Minette's son in law, said:

We were digging around in the Shepard archives and one of the things we found was this incredible photo of Shepard's children Graham and Mary. One the floor by the side of them sits Growler, Graham's teddy bear. The likeness to Winnie-the-Pooh is instantly clear. Although the character Winnie-the-Pooh is based on Christopher Robin Milne's bear, it was Graham's bear Growler that Shepard used as the inspiration for his illustrations of Pooh. Likewise, it was Graham that inspired Shepard's illustrations of Christopher Robin.

To the best of our knowledge this is the only existing photograph of Growler in existence – and we had no idea it was there until we stumbled across it. Shepard was asked by Milne to illustrate his stories in 1926. Shepard was asked to draw a child of about six years old and a bear. He went home and effectively drew what was at home, which was his young son and his son's own teddy.

Christopher Robin Milne's stuffed toys are on display at the New York Public Library and often people are disappointed when they see the bear because it doesn't actually look like Winnie-the-Pooh. You only have to look at this photograph of Growler to see this is the real Winnie-the-Pooh.

Shepard went on to claim that he also based the drawings of Christopher Robin on his own son Graham, saying:

Christopher Robin's legs were too skinny. So I decided to draw my own son, Graham, who was a sturdy little boy. Otherwise I was a stickler for accuracy. All the other illustrations of Christopher Robin and Pooh and Piglet and the other animals were drawn exactly where Milne had visualised them – usually in Ashdown Forest.

But Christopher himself disputed that claim, arguing that Graham was 18 by then: 'It is true that he used his imagination when he drew the animals but me he drew from life. I did indeed look just like that.

Alan eventually persuaded Shepard to visit both the family homes in Chelsea and Hartfield, 'if only to get Pooh and Piglet's likeness'. He was concerned that Piglet needed to be much smaller than the other animals – in the sixth story he is shown jumping up reach the door knocker, and in the seventh he leaps into Kanga's pouch: 'It's hard to be brave when you're a very small animal,' he wrote about the little pig.

John Macrae of Dutton's, Alan's American publisher, described seeing the working partnership in action:

Milne sitting on the sofa reading the story, Christopher Robin sitting on the floor playing with the characters, and, by his side on the floor, sat E.H. Shepard, making sketches for the illustrations which finally went in the book. Christopher Robin, the true inspiration of these four books to both the author and the artist, was entirely unconscious in his part in the drama.

Christopher recalled the process clearly too:

> *It started with me, he said. As I played with them and talked to them and gave them voices to answer with so they began to breathe. But I alone couldn't take them very far. I needed help. So my mother joined me and she and I and the toys played together and gradually more life, more character flowed into them, until they reached a point at which my father could take over. Then, as the first stories were written, the cycle was repeated.*
>
> *Then Shepard came along, looked at the toy Pooh, read the stories and started drawing; and the Pooh who had been developing under my father's pen began to develop under Shepard's pen as well.*

In the Spring of 1926 Shepard was put under great pressure to come up with new illustrations months earlier than anticipated, as the *Royal Magazine* had agreed to publish six of the *Winnie-the-Pooh* short stories prior to the book's publication in October. He was anxious that he would not be able to produce thirteen pictures in time, so Alan negotiated a pay rise for him. It was also his idea that Shepard should receive a share of the sales royalties later, recognising the key role he played in the success of the books. Such a deal was extremely unusual for an illustrator at that time, but Alan made the request to his publishers who drew up new contracts at his insistence. The characters themselves remained Alan's property however, so when rights were granted to reproduce them as toys and other merchandise it was only 'by agreement with the author', and he alone made a fortune.

Alan wrote to Ken: 'Shepard and I are having a joint agreement, dividing in the proportion of 80 to 20. But when I told Daff of the suggested division, 80% to me, 20% to him, she said, "I am sure you make it sound all right to him, but it will want a lot of explanation to Mrs Shepard."'

The two wives met when the whole Shepard family was invited down to farm at Cotchford to give Ernest a chance to explore the setting of the books for himself. Shepard noticed how much more relaxed Alan was when they visited him in the countryside: 'He was a different man,' he said. 'He was quite different, going over the ground and showing me the places.'

Together they all walked up to Gills Lap, the beauty spot that inspired 'the enchanted place on the very top of the forest', and they saw, just as Pooh and Christopher Robin did in the stories, 'the whole world spread out until it reached the sky'. There is now a memorial to them both at that spot. The trees of Ashdown Forest dominate the books, as almost all the characters apart from Rabbit, live in trees, including Christopher Robin himself. Shepard's drawings of a jaunty bear walking through the woods accurately reflect the real scenery, and in another illustration where Piglet is brushing snow away from his door with a tiny broom, the trunk of the beech tree is instantly recognisable. And eagle-eyed visitors to Ashdown Forest can still find a little door in that tree today.

Alan had been initially inspired by an ancient hollow walnut tree in the garden at Cotchford, which had a great open gash in its trunk which seemed to make a door: 'There was plenty of room for a boy and his bear,' Alan said, recalling how Christopher would use the trunk as a perfect sized tree house. Just after his seventh birthday, Alan wrote: 'At the moment he is mad on tree-climbing, which he really does rather well and pluckily, even after doing the last eight feet downwards on his head the other day'.

Shepard's most famous drawing, showing the backs of Christopher Robin, Pooh, and Piglet, watching their sticks float under Poohsticks Bridge – which featured in *Chapter Six: In Which Pooh Invents A New Game And Eeyore Joins In* – has proved such an enduring and iconic image that when the original came up for auction at Sotheby's in December 2014 it sold for an astonishing £314,500. Describing the idyllic scene, Alan wrote: 'For a long time they looked at the river beneath them, saying nothing, and the river said nothing too, for it felt very quiet and peaceful on this summer afternoon'. The drawing, which had been in a private collection for more than forty years, was based on Posingford Bridge at Hartfield Farm. After falling into disrepair in the 1970s the bridge was carefully restored and reopened by Christopher at a ceremony during which he described it as 'as important a bridge as anywhere in the world'.

Although Shepard later claimed that the biggest regret of his life was agreeing to illustrate the stories, as they completely overshadowed all his other work as a painter and cartoonist, he went on to illustrate all four volumes of *Winnie-the-Pooh* stories, as well as Kenneth Grahame's *Wind in the Willows*. He was made an OBE in 1972 in recognition of his illustrations and died on 24 March 1976, age 96. Growler's owner Graham followed in his father's footsteps also becoming an illustrator, but when war broke out he volunteered for the Royal Naval Reserve and was tragically killed in 1942 when his ship, HMS *Polyanthus*, was torpedoed by a Nazi submarine in the mid-Atlantic. His sister Mary was an illustrator too, and provided the pictures for P.L. Travers' *Mary Poppins* books from 1934 to 1988.

When book sales surpassed all expectations, collectors began to make lucrative offers for Alan's original manuscripts. He may have been tempted, but refused to sell and in his will Alan instructed his trustees to donate the handwritten manuscripts of both books to Trinity College, Cambridge, where they are still carefully preserved in archives today.

In the stories, although he is a small child, Christopher Robin is very much the hero, who sensibly refers to books for help at times of crisis and comes to the rescue of his friends. Just as a loving father would, he comforts and protects the animals, takes care of them, and makes sure no harm comes to them. And, like a parent, the toys look up to him as brave and the person to solve all their problems. Alan allowed his character a few moments of weakness, so he did not seem too good to be true, Christopher Robin made occasional slip-ups, and at one point was forced to admit that he had forgotten what the North Pole looks like: 'I did know once,' Christopher Robin says, but it was always Pooh who was more childlike – egotistical, hungry, and boastful.

Christopher was often asked if he could remember the moment he heard the stories for the first time, who read them to him and where they were. How could he forget:

My mother and I were in the drawing room at Cotchford. The door opened and my father came in. "Have you finished it?"
    "I have."
    "May we hear it?"
    My father settled himself in a chair. "Well," he said, "we've had a story about snow and one about the rain, and one about the mist. So I though we ought to have one about the wind. And here it is. It's called In Which Piglet Does A Very Grand Thing. Halfway between Pooh's house and Piglet's house was a thoughtful spot." My mother and I, side by side on the sofa, settled ourselves comfortably, happily, excitedly, to listen.

The entire framework of the first book was based around Christopher Robin's conversations with his father, but apart from Kanga, there was no mother figure for him. Although *Winnie-the-Pooh* was dedicated to Daphne, and Nanny was mentioned many times, the only other mother was a rather undesirable association with the frivolous woman who disappears without her child in the poem *James James Morrison Morrison*.

Years later, writing in *The Spectator*, Ronald Bryden wondered if the mother's absences 'betoken drink, drugs, insanity or infidelity, the child has obviously been driven by some emotional deprivation into a life of lonely fantasy, inventing a series of imaginary playmates'. As a theory, that may have been a little extreme, but clearly not everyone found the characters quite so adorable, and a few literary critics dared to speak their mind, with Chris Powling asking: 'Was there ever a more insufferable child than Christopher Robin?' And Geoffrey Grigson said:

Every inch of him exudes smugness – from the top of that curious, bobbed haircut to the tip of those tiny-tot sandals and the smock and the shorts in between are just as irritating. Christopher Robin must surely be what he seems. And what he seems is a serious affront to anyone who believes children are simply people who haven't lived very long.

CHAPTER FIVE

Luckily for Alan, his son was an early fan of his writing: 'Moon tells me that Pooh is "what I call a good sort of book", which has encouraged me greatly,' Alan said when the books were first published.

Many critics have tried to explain the enduring appeal of the stories. Alison Lurie, who said she saw something of Alan's mother Maria not in Kanga but in Rabbit, suggested that the characters were so universally popular because everyone knew someone like Tigger, Eeyore, Owl, and the others. Humphrey Carpenter also asked: 'Don't we indeed recognise them in ourselves?' It has been suggested many times that we all see ourselves like Pooh, as bears of very little brain trying to bluff our way through life, feeling like everybody else is cleverer, and we would be brave if only we had the chance: 'Hardly anybody knows if those are these or these are those,' as Pooh mused to himself.

Critic Peter Hunt said the stories were: 'The complex work of a complex man, and they include a fascinating series of subtexts that can tell us a lot about the relationships of child, adult, story and book. It is sophisticated writing, the pace, the timing and the narrative stance all contributing to the comic effect'.

The adventures tended to revolve entirely around the things that matter the most to small children – friends, food, birthdays, building dens and tree houses, going on imaginary expeditions, telling jokes and singing songs. No costs were mentioned and the dangers they encountered were natural ones, such as bees, monsters called 'heffalumps', and bad weather. They celebrated moments of community, co-operation and kindness, such as when they worked together to pull Pooh out of the rabbit warren, or rescue Piglet from the flood. The flood story was inspired by a night when Cotchford Farm was surrounded by water but Christopher missed it because he was asleep and Alan said afterwards: 'It wasn't much good having anything exciting like floods, if you couldn't share them with somebody'.

Just as the world was falling in love with the characters, the appeal was beginning to wear thin for Christopher Robin himself. He started to wonder if perhaps his father wrote about him to avoid having to engage with him in real life:

People often say to me: "How lucky you were to have such a wonderful father!" imagining that because he wrote about me with such affection and understanding, he must have played with me with equal affection and understanding. Can this really be so untrue? Isn't this most surprising?

No, it is not really surprising, not when you understand. There are two sorts of writer. There is the writer who is basically a reporter and there is the creative writer. The one draws on his experiences, the other on his dreams. My father was a creative writer and so it was precisely because he was not able to play with his small son that his longings sought and found satisfaction in another direction. He wrote about him instead.

His new-found fame meant Alan was often being interviewed, and there were many descriptions of the house at Mallord Street which was said to be immaculately decorated, and lots of references to his good looks, his great sense of humour, his modesty, charm, and of course his enchanting son. Christopher said later: 'I quite liked being Christopher Robin and being famous. There were indeed times when it was exciting and made me feel grand and important'.

It was only much later that he would grow up to resent the books so fiercely, as gradually the outside world began to creep in, although Alan saw no reason to protect his son from the publicity, while Daphne seemed to positively encourage the press. They were confident that it would not affect his life at home or school in any adverse way, and when he was 6, his grandfather John wrote: 'Alan's boy is quite unspoilt. He complains that school is easier than ever, but Alan thinks he learns quite enough. He makes up for it by learning chess and whist at home!'

And for many years growing up in public did not affect the happy relationship that had blossomed between Alan and his teenage son, as they maintained great admiration for one another. Describing his father, Christopher said: 'These really, were his two great talents: perfectionism and enthusiasm. He handed them on to me – and he could have given me nothing more'.

By 1926 Alan found himself in great demand. He received many offers from the BBC to read his poems and stories aloud on the radio, but he felt insulted by the low fees on offer, and sent a furious article to the *Evening News* complaining about the way writers were being treated:

Authors have never been taken seriously by their fellow man, he wrote. *The attitude seems to be a painter is a painter and a sculptor sculpts but dash it all, a writer only writes, which is a thing we all do every day of our lives, and the only difference between ourselves and Thomas Hardy is that Hardy doesn't do anything else, whereas we are busy men with a real job of work to do.*

You would not hesitate to ask an author for a free article for some ephemeral publication in which you were interested, or for permission to perform his play without the usual payment of royalty. Indeed you would feel that you were paying him the same sort of compliment that I should be paying you if dining at your house, I asked to see the soap dish in your bathroom.

Now the BBC exploits to its highest power this attitude of kindly condescension to the author. To the BBC all authors are the same author.

Alan was angry at the low amount he had been offered to read something for a special Gala Night, and instead of coming back with a higher figure, he claimed someone at the *BBC* had argued: 'Not even for the sake of the Little Ones?'

His article went on:

There is a 'regular fee' for the author, whoever he is, and with any luck the BBC can avoid paying even this ridiculous amount by an ingenious scheme of its own. It says to the author, "If we pay you a fee, we won't mention your name or your works or your publishers or anything about you, but if you will let us do it for nothing we will announce to our thousand million book buying listeners where your book is to be bought. And if you don't like it, you can leave it, because there are plenty of other authors about; and, if it came to the worst, we could write the things ourselves quite easily."'

This spectacular and very public falling out with the BBC did nothing to dent his popularity however, and a film producer tried to persuade Alan to allow cameras to follow him at work, for what would have been one of the very earliest reality television programmes. Alan explained to Ken what scenes they had hoped to film: 'Entering the Library after Kissing Wife Farewell, Deep In Thought, Interrupted by Prattling Child, Takes Child on Knee and Pats Head of Same, Sudden Inspiration, Throws Child Away and Seizes Pen, Writes, Fade Out'. Evidently Alan loathed the idea, although the producer tried to argue that it would have educational benefits for aspiring authors. Alan also turned down an offer from Pears Soap who wanted him to write a story featuring their product. He allowed the advertising executives to buy him a lavish dinner at The Ritz and even gave them a tour of his London townhouse, but ultimately he was not impressed. The makers of Wolsey children's underwear also made him a generous offer, but Alan was even less interested in underwear than soap: 'The story would be left entirely to Mr Milne,' they urged. 'Subject only to there being included in it some, so to speak, fatherly remarks upon the warmth and wisdom of children being underclothed in wool.'

That summer Christopher Robin became a schoolboy, and started attending Miss Walters' School in Tite Street, a short walk from their house in Chelsea: 'Billy loves his school,' Alan wrote to Ken. 'Though I never quite know what he is doing. He brings home weird works of art from time to time, hand-painted pottery and what not, which has to be disposed of by Daff.'

CHAPTER FIVE

By the time he was six, Christopher was no longer interested in toy bears, preferring to study a map of Africa which hung on his wall, and the *Children's Encyclopedia* which he carried everywhere with him. Stunned to learn that he would be packed off to boarding school when he reached the age of 10, Christopher asked his father, who by this stage he was calling Blue: 'Do I ever come back to you after that?' And since he was becoming passionate about wildlife, Christopher decided that he would rather become an elephant hunter instead, but Alan said: 'I can't bear to think of him being trodden on by an elephant'. As far as Alan was concerned, it was impossible for anyone with a sense of humour to be a strict father: 'The necessary assumption of authority and wisdom seems so ridiculous,' he said. 'Over and over again you hear the threat "If you do that again I'll punish you," and if he does it again, how can we help admiring his pluck, seeing how small he is and how big we are.'

As an adult, Christopher agreed that his father never stuck to the rules:

He could teach and loved teaching. He could radiate enthusiasm but he could never impose discipline. He could never have taught a dull subject to a dull boy, never have said "Do this because I say so." My father's relationships were always between equals, however old or young, distinguished or undistinguished the other person.

Alan once attempted to scold his son for sitting at the lunch table with his knife and fork pointing upwards but ended up saying: 'Suppose somebody suddenly fell through the ceiling. They might land on your fork and that would be very painful'.

CHAPTER SIX

'This writing business. Pencils and what-not. Over-rated, if you ask me. Silly stuff. Nothing in it.'

Winnie-The-Pooh was published on 14 October 1926 in London, and in New York a week later, but this time Alan was slightly better prepared for the inevitable success when it came. Critics on both sides of the Atlantic were astonished that he had been able to pull off the rare coup of striking gold once again with a second book. A review in *The New York Herald Tribune* gushed: 'There are not so very many books that, sitting reading all alone, you find yourself laughing aloud over. This is one of them. Here is nonsense in the best tradition, with the high seriousness about it that children and other wise people love'.

Vogue magazine declared: 'It has tremendous charm and is great fun to read aloud'. Like the first book, it appealed to adults as much as children. By the end of the year, 150,000 copies had been sold in the United States: 'In America, by the way, they seem at least twice as keen as they were on *WWWVY*,' remarked Alan. And his British publishers Methuen were so confident of having a bestselling sequel on their hands that the initial print run was seven times the size of *When We Were Very Young*. On publication day, bookshops up and down the country were filled with 32,000 special copies bound in green cloth, followed by a further 3,000 bound in red, blue or green leather, as well as other commemorative editions aimed at book collectors. The following year the print run for *Now We Are Six* would be 50,000 and for *The House At Pooh Corner* it was 75,000. Within a very short space of time the four children's books had been reprinted into dozens of languages and sales were soaring into the millions.

Alan had every reason to be delighted with himself, and made it clear there was more to come by paving the way for a sequel at the end of *Winnie-the-Pooh*:

> *"And what did happen?" Asked Christopher Robin.*
> *"I don't know."*
> *"Could you think, and tell me and Pooh sometime?"*
> *"If you wanted it very much."*
> *"Pooh does," said Christopher Robin.*

Among the mountains of praise, fan mail and requests for articles, appearances and autographs that began to pile up on his desk, Alan also began to receive begging letters from worthy, and sometimes not so worthy, causes. He tried to be charitable, making a point of supporting less successful writers such as Edwin Pugh, and donating generously to the Royal Literary Fund and the Society of Authors Pension Fund. He often said how easy it was to give money, but much more difficult to actually do something practical to help people who were worse off.

Although he very rarely attended charity events, and disliked public speaking, Alan would often agree to write appeal letters and penned several successful fund-raising requests for the Children's Country Holiday Fund, which were published in *The Times*: 'Ladies may regret their last hat, and a man the new brassie which has not added twenty yards to his drive. The only money which we are never sorry to have spent is the money which we have given away,' he wrote. Alan gave away a percentage of his own earnings, having put his own financial success down to sheer good fortune, and once remarked:

> *Idiots we are, if we can look at ourselves, however high our achievements, however great our success, with anything but humility and thankfulness. Our achievements, our possessions, are not of our own making; they were given to us. There is only one honest answer to that hackneyed question of the interviewer: "To what do you attribute your success?" And that answer is "Luck!"*

And luckily for Alan, he had plenty of cash to spare, although he chose not to splash it around in any particularly ostentatious ways. Both his London and Sussex homes were beautifully furnished and adequately staffed with servants, he had a car with a chauffeur, and he paid all the school fees and medical expenses for Ken's family. But their wealth never sat comfortably with Christopher who once remarked: 'There was something not quite nice about being rich'. Alan had reached a stage in his life where he could happily enjoy extravagances without having to worry about the costs, but they were usually minor ones: 'We set our standards within our income and then enjoyed them carelessly,' he said. 'I shouldn't be happy if I couldn't be reckless about golf balls, taxis, the best seats at cricket grounds and theatres, shirts and pullovers, tips, subscriptions, books and wine lists.' One thing he did enjoy spending lavishly on was expensive lingerie for Daphne, which he would choose carefully from Harvey Nichols in Knightsbridge, describing his purchases as: 'Soft, pretty crepe-de-chiney, lacey things. What fun!'

Alan never gambled, but invested cautiously in a number of well-selected, worthwhile projects. In 1928 he was among the key financial backers for his friend P.G. Wodehouse's dramatisation of his novel *A Damsel In Distress*. But Alan always feared the money would run out, that one day people would stop buying his books, and so he never stopped looking for fresh ideas.

As plans for the next instalment of the series, *Now We Are Six*, began to take shape in his mind, he revisited the adorable friendship between Christopher Robin and his beloved bear leading to one of his most famous and enduring verses called *Us Two*:

Wherever I am, there's always Pooh,
There's always Pooh and Me.
Whatever I do, he wants to do,
"Where are you going today?" says Pooh:
"Well, that's very odd 'cos I was too.
"Let's go together," says Pooh, says he.
"Let's go together," says Pooh.

CHAPTER SIX

With poems such as *King John's Christmas* and *Sneezles*, when *Now We Are Six* was published on 13 October 1928, many felt it was even better than *When We Were Very Young*. According to *The Retail Bookseller* it was: 'Another unquestionable bulls eye. For the third time A.A. Milne has demonstrated that a book for children can outsell'. An instant hit, within two months of publication it had already overtaken the best-selling *Winnie-The-Pooh,* which had been published a year earlier. Among the scores of rave reviews was one very outspoken critic, the author Dorothy Parker, who wrote a scathing piece in the *New Yorker* saying:

> *There is a strong feeling I know, that to speak against Mr Milne puts one immediately in the ranks of those who set fire to orphanages, strike crippled newsboys, and lure little curly heads into corners to explain to them that Santa Claus is only Daddy making a fool of himself. But I too have a strong feeling about the Whimsicality of Milne. I'm feeling it right this minute. It's in my stomach.*

Even some of Alan's most dedicated admirers found the book's sugary dedication rather nauseating: 'To Anne Darlington, now she is seven and because she is so speshal,' he had written. Anne had been there when the stories first took shape, and remembered Alan speaking to the toys in the nursery as if they were real people, although her father claimed that it had actually been Daphne who gave the animals their unique characters, while Alan 'never joined in the games but watched them with delight'. A reporter called Claude Luke gave readers further insight into the family dynamic when he visited the house in Chelsea and asked Christopher whether he liked his father's books: 'He gazed at me for a moment, amazed at the immense foolishness of humans and then turned to his nurse with the expressive remark, "Do I Nanny?" as though to say, "Throw out this absurd man."'

Christopher confirmed that his mother would play with the toys more than Alan ever did, although he would end up with most of the credit:

Gradually more life, more character flowed into them, until they reached a point at which my father could take over, he said. Then as the first stories were written, the cycle was repeated. The Pooh in my arms, the Pooh sitting opposite me at the breakfast table was a Pooh who had climbed trees in search of honey, who had got stuck in a rabbit hole.

Alan dedicated the final stories to Daphne in a romantic poem which she treasured, thanking her for playing those games with their son, which had so inspired him:

> *You gave me Christopher Robin, and then*
> *You breathed new life in Pooh.*
> *Whatever of each has left my pen*
> *Goes homing back to you.*
> *My book is ready, and comes to greet*
> *The mother it longs to see –*
> *It would be my present to you, my sweet,*
> *If it weren't your gift to me.*

Not long after *The House At Pooh Corner* was published in London, and then New York in October 1928, it became another instant bestseller, and readers were warned that this would be the final instalment. A review in *Punch* said: 'The last book is as good as the first. It is too bad that Christopher Robin has to grow up'. And the *Saturday Review* added: 'The stories have lost none of their charm. It is a shame to see them end'. But Dorothy Parker, writing under the pseudonym of the Constant Reader, wrote another scathing critique, this time of Pooh's hum called 'The more it snows tiddly pom'. She wrote: 'It is that word hummy, my darlings, that marks the first place in *The House At Pooh Corner* at which Tonstant Weader fwowed up'.

The same month the book was published Christopher started at prep school, Gibbs in Sloane Square, and while his innocence was not completely shattered, cracks started to show. Christopher's life would never be the same again as he began to realise just how very famous he was. The boy whose name had become so very notorious was leaving behind the sanctity of his nursery and the forest, and was struggling to come to terms with his phenomenal popularity, whether he liked it or not. Just as Christopher Robin explained to his faithful friend Pooh at the end of the book, his carefree days were behind him: 'I'm not going to do Nothing any more'. 'Never again?' 'Well not so much. They don't let you.'

Alan agreed to let Christopher be recorded reciting several of the poems, saying: 'He loves it, is quite unshy, and speaks beautifully'. But that was a decision which would come back to haunt them both in years to come. When he was a teenager at Stowe School in Buckinghamshire, and the bullying was beyond control, other boys played that recording of him reading *Vespers* over and over again, taunting him mercilessly until one day he could take the cruelty no more: 'Eventually the joke, if not the record, wore out, they handed it to me,' Christopher recalled. 'I took it and broke it into a hundred fragments and scattered them over a distant field. Boys, after all, can be pretty beastly to each other when they try.' His cousin Angela, equally scarred by the trauma, supported Christopher by hanging the record from a tree and allowing her children to throw things at it.

When he finally stopped writing about Christopher Robin in 1929, Alan felt the need to defend his decision, claiming to be shocked that his son had become far more famous than he could have ever imagined. In a lengthy essay entitled *The End of A Chapter* he wrote:

You can imagine my amazement and disgust when I discovered that I had been pushed into a back place, and that the hero of When We Were Very Young was not, as I had modestly expected, the author, but a curiously named child. It was this Christopher Robin who kept mice, walked on the lines and not in the squares, and wondered what to do on a spring morning; it was this Christopher Robin, not I, whom Americans were clamouring to see.

To me he was, and remained, the child of my imagination.

When I thought of him, I thought of him in the Forest, living in his tree as no child really lives, not in the nursery where a differently named child (so far as we in this house are concerned) was playing with his animals. For this reason I have not felt self-conscious when writing about him, nor apologetic at the thought of exposing my own family to public gaze. The animals are a different case. I have exploited them for my own profit, as I feel I have not exploited the legal Christopher Robin. All I have got from Christopher Robin is a name which he never uses, an introduction to his friends, and a gleam which I have tried to follow.

This then brings me to one of the reasons why these verses and stories have come to an end. I feel that the legal Christopher Robin has already had more publicity than I want for him. Moreover, since he is growing up, he will soon feel that he has had more publicity than he wants for himself. We all, young and old, hope to make some sort of name, but we want to make it in our own chosen way, and if possible, by our own exertions.

Lawrence hid himself in the Air Force under the name of Shaw to avoid being introduced for the rest of his life as Lawrence of Arabia. I do not want C.R. Milne ever to wish that his names were Charles Robert. I have had my thrill out of children's books, he concluded. And I know that I will never recapture it. At least, not until I am a grandfather.

Sadly, Alan would never know how it felt to be a grandfather as his only grandchild Clare was only born, severely disabled, a few months after he died.

CHAPTER SEVEN

'If there ever comes a day when we can't be together keep me in your heart, I'll stay there forever.'

Shortly after *The House At Pooh Corner* was published, Ken's health took another turn for the worse, and his tuberculosis left him confined to bed. Alan was paying for the best medical advice and treatment available at the time, but there was nothing more to be done, and he was devastated when his older brother died on 21 May 1929 at the age of just 48. The funeral was held at St Peter and St John the Baptist Church at Wivelsfield, near their parent's home in Sussex, but Alan was not at the service. He could not bring himself to sit among the weeping mourners in the church, but nor he could not bear to stay away. Ken's children remembered glimpsing him standing alone in the churchyard, lost in his thoughts among the gravestones, wearing his best blue suit.

Alan was utterly bereft and never fully recovered from the loss of the brother he had adored so much. He could not find the words to write about his grief, although some years later he did dedicate his autobiography to the memory of Ken: 'Who bore the worst of me and made the best of me'.

He never forgot the promises he had made Ken, vowing to always provide for his family, and Alan shouldered the entire financial responsibility for his widow Maud and their four bereaved children. Both of Ken's sons followed the family tradition and were attending Westminster School so Alan encouraged Maud and her daughters Marjorie and Angela to move back to London from Somerset, to be closer to the boys, and found them a house in Gledhow Gardens, a short walk from his own home in Chelsea: 'She is full of fight,' Alan told his father about Maud. 'She has no intention of sitting down and doing nothing.' Maud and Daphne were never really friends, and only met very occasionally, but Alan remained close to his sister-in-law and supported her for the rest of her life. He was also very generous with Barry's wife Connie, who suffered money worries too.

He was still engulfed by grief for Ken when the time came for Alan to say goodbye to Christopher and his nanny too. With Christopher heading off to boarding school, they no longer required the services of Olive Rand who left to get married – after postponing her wedding for several years to care for Christopher. Alan's present to Olive was a cottage, which she called *Vespers*, although by then it was too late for her to have children of her own. It was a time of great upheaval for Alan, and no longer able to write to Ken, he began to send long handwritten letters to his son at school instead.

He took it badly when his latest play *The Ivory Door* was a flop, closing its doors after just twenty performances, and as if all that were not bad enough, it looked as if Alan's marriage might be drifting apart as well. Gloomily, Alan feared he had been irrevocably labelled as 'whimsical' after the *Pooh* stories, and there was precious little he could do about it, if he complained he was accused of being ungrateful for his success:

I have the Whimsical label so firmly round my own neck that I can neither escape from it nor focus it, he fumed. It seems to me now that if I write anything less realistic, less straightforward than "The cat sat on the mat" I am "indulging in whimsy". The Ivory Door is damned and slammed not by the public but by the critics.

The New Yorker called it: 'A lethal combination of whimsy and lethargy,' and Alan was forced to accept he had his first real failure on his hands. He wrote to E.V. Lucas: 'The critics damned it as if it were worse than the worst film you have seen (one can't go lower than that) and Daff and I have been feeling terribly sunk, because we loved it childishly'.

He went on to publicly moan about the practice of critics always reviewing a new production on its first night, as the cast were often ill-prepared, but his complaints fell on deaf ears: 'The first night is critical, often too critical to receive the brunt of critical judgment,' he argued. Alan was so angry he threatened to abandon the theatre altogether: 'We can do without each other,' he warned. But of course, he could not do without the theatre, and soon started working on another play, *Michael and Mary*, which would turn out be his last real stage success. His private life was not faring particularly well either, he was spending more and more time away from London and away from Daphne, as he found ideas were not flowing as freely as they once did, and felt there were less distractions in the countryside: 'I dread this interval between one idea and another,' he confessed. 'My trouble now is not too many ideas, but an almost total absence of them.'

Michael and Mary was an exploration of a troubled marriage which started rumours swirling about him and his own wife, but he wrote to his father to reassure him that everything was fine between them: 'We have been, and are, terribly happy together. She is a perpetual joy to me and I think I am to her'. But if he sounded rather uncertain in that letter, it was because over the next decade Alan and Daphne would lead increasingly separate lives.

She had always been hugely enthusiastic about the *Pooh* stories, something which became a major cause of conflict between them after Alan said he wished he had never written them. At the height of his success, Daphne had delighted in acting as Alan's secretary, answering letters from all over the world, taking care of visitors who begged to see Christopher Robin's nursery, and arranging their busy social calendar. She appeared to be the perfect spouse, particularly in an interview when she advised other women to put their husbands first, just as she had apparently always done:

A successful wife just simply cannot be too egotistical, and modern women are cultivating their egos too strongly. I honestly think the only really successful marriage, disregarding the few exceptions that prove the rule, is that in which the wife is interested only in her husband and his career – I mean in which that career dominates her whole life, and is the thing she really lives for.

Publicly Daphne was always very careful not to reveal anything other than romantic bliss: 'He has a most even and genial disposition,' she added. 'He makes life very interesting and amusing for us. He doesn't save up his best thoughts for strangers.'

In private however, Daphne was far from a traditional housewife. While Alan wanted to retreat away from prying eyes, Daphne would never be satisfied by a quiet life and soon there came a time when, as Alan put it, they were both 'marginally in love with other people'. While they both discovered happiness with someone else behind closed doors, they still managed to keep their marriage intact, divorce never seemed to be an option for them: 'The secret of a loving marriage is to have a partner to whom you don't have to explain things,' Alan said. 'I didn't say a happy marriage. I said a loving marriage.'

In his play *Mr Pim Passes By*, Alan showed that he was years ahead of his time when it came to equality:

I shall try to remember that marriage is a partnership, in which the man is not inevitably the senior partner, he wrote. *I bring my wife no less than I receive from her. I expect from her no more than I can keep for her. In this matter, I recognise no shadow of a difference between the two sexes.*

As he came to accept the highly unconventional nature of his relationship with Daphne, Alan revealed yet more of his feelings in an essay called *Love and Marriage* which examined how traditional domestic roles were gradually starting to change as women fought for greater equality, and an end to servitude:

Man is suddenly in the horrible position of realising that 'a happy marriage' in some ridiculous way has got to mean

*happiness for the woman also. Is it any wonder that there is
this rush of unhappy marriages? What would happen to all the
shooting parties each autumn if they had suddenly to include
happiness for a vocal pheasant?*

Alan no longer needed to work for money, he had given up journalism
and writing poetry almost entirely, and with Christopher packed off to
boarding school, Daphne was determined to forge a new life for
herself. She had plenty of time on her hands and sought out new
friends and ways of entertaining herself. Alan had grown tired of
travelling, and when he and Daphne travelled to America in October
1931, it was the last trip they made together – although she would
return again and again without him. As a couple they were much in
demand by the cream of high society in New York, and among the
torrent of invitations came one that would change everything for Alan
and Daphne – the playwright Elmer Rice asked to entertain them in
his Manhattan apartment one evening. They had previously been
introduced when he was in London for the production of his play *Street
Scene,* which had scooped a prestigious Pulitzer Prize award. Alan was
a great fan of Rice's, he admired both his politics and his writing, and
even paid tribute to his work in the preface to *Michael and Mary –*
comparing his plays to Shakespeare's *Hamlet*.

While most of New York society was keen to show the Milnes the
glitzier side of life in the Big Apple, Rice wanted to give them a dose
of reality. Their visit came two years after the Wall Street crash and
the gulf between rich and poor in the city had never been wider. Rice
refused to ignore the effects of the depression, which left people
queuing at soup kitchens, begging for bread and sleeping rough in the
parks, even in November. He came from a poor Jewish background
himself, having been born with the surname Reizenstein, he changed
it to Rice to avoid persecution. As a child he experienced great hunger
and poverty, and shared a bedroom with his grandfather. As a result,
despite his enormous success in the theatre, he never lost his passion
for social justice, which impressed Alan enormously. Daphne had
certainly never met anyone like him before.

Rice's first play explored feminist themes, and he described the second, which was called *The Seventh Commandment* as 'an attack on the social code that condemns in a woman what is condones in a man'. By the time he was just 21 he was enjoying a hugely successful career, his third play *On Trial* earned him a staggering $100,000, and he was amassing a collection of valuable paintings by artists including Picasso, Leger, and Modigliani. But despite his elevated social status, he remained passionate about socialist politics, was a pacifist and an ardent supporter of women's rights. He was an active member of the American Civil Liberties Union, the National Council on Freedom from Censorship and the Dramatists Guild. In his autobiography, he said he always managed to somehow retain: 'A kind of romantic idealism and a feeling that life is potentially good, that people are potentially trustworthy'. He and Alan clearly had a great deal in common, but it was Daphne who fell the hardest for his charms. She was said to be utterly besotted by the tall redhead, and although she had many other friends in America, it was Rice who drew her back to New York many times over the next few years.

She would see him in London too; but Alan was far from a cuckolded husband, hardly waiting at home alone nursing a broken heart. While Daphne was spending time with Rice, he was forging a close relationship with a young actress called Leonora Corbett, whom he first met when she played the part of Delia in a revival of his play *Belinda* at the Embassy Theatre in Swiss Cottage, North London. And he got to know her much better after he put her forward for the lead role of Lola Waite in his new play *Other People's Lives* in November 1932 at the Arts Theatre in London. It seemed Daphne had her husband's consent to travel alone, and to quietly build a private life of her own. Although she publicly talked of the dangers of 'modern women cultivating their egos too strongly,' their unusual marital arrangements soon became an open secret among Manhattan's highest social circles.

The *New York Post* newspaper reported:

Auburn-haired Mrs. A.A. Milne, wife of the novelist and playwright arrived on the Aquitania today for what she called "my annual vacation from my husband". Smiling she told ship news reporters: "Sometimes I act as his secretary and do all sorts of tasks for him – so he thinks I ought to have a rest from him once a year. I'll stay a month, go to the theatres – and see his producers! Still working for him, you see."

Daphne regularly rented an apartment at the exclusive Lombardy Hotel overlooking Central Park on East Fifty Sixth Street, for several weeks at time. She felt that New York offered her the sort of glamour, romance and glittering lifestyle which she had always enjoyed but no longer shared with her husband. 'She got a bit bored with him,' one of her friends revealed later. 'Women need someone else – she used to say – to take them out to lunch and spoil them.'

Many observers wondered what Rice, an imaginative realist, could have in common with an eternal optimist who viewed her entire life cheerfully through rose-tinted spectacles. But many men were drawn to Daphne, and there was no denying her great wit and charm. The actress Fabia Drake later described her 'extraordinary gaiety, her brightness and warmth, which attracted many people'.

Rice, who took a notoriously controversial stance when it came to his 'outside attachments' with various women, never officially confirmed anything more scandalous than a very close friendship with Mrs Milne. But a revealing passage in his autobiography, referring specifically to this time when he was with Daphne, suggested that his wife Hazel Levy and Alan were both aware of the relationship but accepted it, or chose to turn a blind eye, for many years:

Since I had not found within my marriage the satisfactions I sought, I had either to forgo them, terminate my marriage or seek to supply its deficiencies elsewhere. The third course seemed the best, he wrote. I had no moral compulsion to monogamy. It is my belief that man is not by nature a monogamous animal. In general, statutes making adultery a crime are seldom enforced.

To me sexual fidelity seemed a personal, pragmatic matter, like a belief in God or life after death. Its validity depended upon whether or not it worked for you. I think that when a man and woman find complete emotional satisfaction in each other fidelity becomes a matter of course. That was certainly true of my second marriage. But on that basis the first would never have survived.

It did survive for another twenty years, during which I always had outside attachments. I did not flaunt these relationships, nor did I discuss them with my wife; but I was not furtive about them either. Indeed she was often inclined to suspect intimacy where none existed. The fact that she did not seek a divorce is evidence, I think, that for her too the maintenance of a home and the pleasures of family life outweighed other considerations. Of course I conceded to her the same freedom I demanded for myself; nor did I protest when she availed herself of it. Fortunately for myself and for others, my many faults do not include possessiveness and sexual jealousy. I have been hurt and angered by spiritual betrayal, but physical infidelity has never disturbed me.

Since I am no Casanova, eager to parade his conquests, I shall I have little more to say on this subject. In fact my love relationships were not conquests at all. I did not go about seeking adventures; but neither did I reject opportunities when they offered themselves. I never made advances unless I had reason to believe they would be welcome if I found I was mistaken, I desisted.

Some of these relationships were transitory, the spontaneous expression of mutual attraction. Others, deeply charged with emotion, went on for years. None, however casual, was sordid, tawdry or mercenary. Some of my partners were married, others not; almost without exception they were women of superior intelligence, talent, sensitivity and character. Over the years these attachments were a source of stimulation and contributed immeasurably to my understanding of myself and other people.

Daphne was certainly one of Rice's 'attachments', and their close relationship lasted for several years, possibly until he met his second wife Betty Field. Later Daphne admitted to one of Alan's nieces how much it had hurt when Rice was no longer interested in her. And Fabia Drake said that Daphne wished things had been rather different: 'I think Daphne regretted having followed his own path of infidelity,' she said, but other family members have agreed that it was Daphne, not Alan, who cheated first. Daphne also confided in another friend that she regretted never apologising to her husband for those long periods when she was away with Rice in America. But Alan seemed to accept the situation entirely, and did not try to conceal her absences, at a time when it was still extremely rare for wives to take any sort of trips without their husbands. In a rhyming response to his friend John Drinkwater who had invited the Milnes for Sunday lunch at his house in Mortimer Crescent, the street where he had grown up in north London, Alan revealed that his wife was amusing herself elsewhere:

> *I'd love to come and see you one day*
> *But cannot ever manage Sunday.*
> *In Sussex, that enchanted spot,*
> *I have a little weekend cot*
> *Intended, as one might deduce,*
> *For Saturday to Monday use.*
> *P.S. Perhaps I ought to say*
> *My wife is in the U.S.A*
> *If not she would be sending*
> *Her thanks, and apologies, and ending*
> *My letter this November P.M.*
> *Yours jointly A.A.M. and D.M.*

Although it was widely known that the couple were living separate lives, and there was a great deal of gossip circulating about what went on behind closed doors, this letter shows how important it still was to Alan to put on a united front to the world.

There was fevered speculation whenever he was spotted dining with Leonora at one of his favourite West End restaurants, either The Ivy or Mirabelle, although their romance was widely accepted open secret among the theatrical community: 'The Leonora Corbett affair was well known,' Fabia Drake said. Leonora's first appearance in Alan's play *Other People's Lives* at the Arts Theatre in London coincided neatly with Daphne's first solo trip to New York in October 1932. Playing Lola Waite, one of the bright young things who decides to intervene in the lives of their pathetic neighbours, she received very mixed reviews: 'Leonora Corbett behaved in her usual cool and detached manner, which occasionally was marred by awkward movements,' said one.

Leonora was exceptionally attractive, and Alan found it a curious experience hearing her say the lines he had written. Some critics suggested that the dialogue he wrote for *Two People* was his way of telling Leonora how he felt about her: 'You did rather get me tonight. I do like intelligence in a woman, provided she's got a certain amount of looks. Of course I know that the things you said tonight weren't your own...indeed they were mine. But you do say things like that pretty often'.

Alan's niece Angela said Leonora spoke her uncle's language, and that she was just as amusing and quick-witted as he was. The actor Griffith Jones described her as 'enchanting, witty, elegant and sexy,' adding that she used her good looks to further her career. He remembered Leonora saying: 'No-one can accuse me of having got here by my acting'. He also claimed that a cousin of hers once said: 'Leonora is naughty and can be dangerous, but she has a heart'.

Another actor Godfrey Kenton also remembered Leonora as 'witty and intelligent' and recalled that there was also gossip circulating that she was having an affair with A.R. Whatmore, who directed her in the role of Delia Tremayne in a revival of Alan's play *Belinda* at the Embassy Theatre. Whatmore would go on to direct Leonora several more times during the 1930s, and they appeared on stage together too. Perhaps unsurprisingly, Alan had a very low opinion of Whatmore, particularly his acting talents: 'He played Tremayne at the Embassy and was very bad,' he wrote to his friend Irene Vanburgh. Alan tried to derail plans for Whatmore to play the same part again in the celebration of Irene's jubilee on the stage in 1938.

By then Leonora had gone on to star in yet another of Alan's plays, *Sarah Simple*, and her reputation as a playwright's muse made her the subject of some cutting remarks made by writer Louis MacNeice about the state of morality at the time:

> *I see England in the Thirties as a chaos of unhappy or dreary marriages, banal or agonised affairs, he wrote. The pattern of every night shot through with the pounding or jiggling of bedsteads, but somewhere in the hearts of the couples on the beds is a reedy little voice of enquiry: "Is this enough?" Or "Is this what I really want?" Or "Can this possibly go on?" Freud having taught my generation that sex repression is immoral, fornication had become a virtue. It remained to discover that neither fornication nor chastity is an end in itself.*

But Alan was among those in England living for the moment, and once said: 'Don't miss any happiness that is going or you'll find it gone'. He added that as an adult, happiness is 'tainted with the knowledge that it will not last, and the fear that one will have to pay for it'. Although the letters exchanged between Alan and Leonora have since been destroyed, they did not conceal their relationship, and Fabia Drake said: 'Daphne knew of his infidelities and they hurt her'. They even went so far as to attend a number of public and family occasions as a couple. Indeed, Leonora was among the esteemed guests when Alan gave an intimate lunch party in a private apartment at the Garrick Club in 1936. The other writers who were invited that day, including Peter Llewellyn Davies, Harry Graham, and Roland Pertwee, brought their wives.

Ken's children also met Leonora several times and thought of her as 'a counter-blast to Daphne's activities in New York'. Angela described her as 'one of nature's tie-straighteners', as she recalled her 'straightening Alan's tie or his collar or something', in a rather proprietorial manner. Alan and Leonora remained extremely close until 1941 when she went to New York to play Elvira in Noel Coward's play *Blithe Spirit* and never returned to England. Alan did not see her again, and while that romance was clearly of huge importance to Alan, his marriage somehow weathered the storm and survived intact. Both he and Daphne accepted the situation as it was, and managed to maintain a great deal of affection and tenderness for each other until the very end.

It was an unusual arrangement, and a far cry from the sort of marriage his parents had – his mother and father were once described by their family friend Biddie Warren as 'sweethearts to the very end.' But perhaps as a result of living very separate lives much of the time, Alan and Daphne appeared to get along a great deal better than many couples, and they were always glad to see each other. Daphne still laughed at her husband's jokes, they adored spending time in the garden at Cotchford together, and of course they were both utterly devoted to Christopher, even if Daphne rarely visited him at school. Because of her long periods away, Alan usually turned up by himself to cheer Christopher on at prize giving days or cricket matches, both at Boxgrove and later at Stowe. As a result the relationship between Christopher and his mother became increasingly detached, and it was always Alan who drove him back to school after visits home, giving them extra time alone:

> *The goodbye I said to my father was different from the one I had said an hour earlier to my mother*, Christopher recalled. *Hers was goodbye until the next holidays. His was only a partial goodbye; for part of him would be remaining with me, hovering over me, lovingly and anxiously watching me throughout the term. It was he, far more often than she, who used to visit me on visiting days; he who knew the masters; he who could chat happily and naturally to the other boys.*

Christopher was eager to please his father, and could not bear disappointing his high expectations. He vividly recalled Alan coming to watch him play in a school cricket match when he was bowled out early, before scoring a single run:

My father had always hoped that one day I would be a great cricketer, captaining the Stowe Eleven perhaps, or even playing for Cambridge. But at Stowe the tender plant that had been so devotedly nourished hour after hour at wickets during the holidays drooped and faded: I got no further than the Third Eleven.

Gradually Alan stopped discussing Christopher's mediocre achievements on the cricket pitch, and in any case his dear friend Turley, who had been the recipient of so many boastful letters about Christopher, died the following year. And some years later, Alan would deny all the talent Christopher had apparently shown for the sport as a small boy. When he heard that his great-niece, Marjorie's daughter Alison, had bowled him out in a game Alan was highly dismissive of his skills, saying:

I have played with him in a net for hours and weeks and years, and I doubt if he bowled a ball inside the net more than three times, and then only by hitting one of the posts first and bouncing inside. So he must have improved a good deal – or perhaps he was bowling underhand.

Regardless of his sporting achievements, Alan's favourite dining companion was always his son. He would take any opportunity to whisk Christopher off for dinner at The Ivy, or they would travel by bus for a lunch of scrambled eggs or baked beans on toast at the ABC restaurant on the King's Road: 'When the holidays were over and I was back at school, his first letter to me would recall that happy lunch that he and I had had together. He and I – and the ghost of Ken,' Christopher said.

CHAPTER EIGHT

'If you live to be a hundred, I want to live to be a hundred minus one day, so I never have to live without you.'

No matter how hard he tried, Alan was unable to escape what he now saw as the curse of being a famous children's author. On top of *Winnie-the-Pooh*'s enduring success, by the end of 1930, after almost a decade of waiting, his adaptation of Kenneth Grahame's much loved tale *The Wind In The Willows* was finally making its debut in London's West End. From its opening night onwards, *Toad of Toad Hall* was declared a massive triumph, and immediately established itself alongside the likes of *Peter Pan* and *Alice in Wonderland* as a classic family favourite. *Toad* remains the only one of Alan's plays that is still frequently produced today.

Alan did his best to attend almost all the rehearsals as he was keen to ensure the play's success, although he was disappointed when critics drew inevitable comparisons between *Pooh* and *Toad*: 'The Wild Wood is quite evidently only a mile or two away from the Forest in which dwell Mr Milne's own creations,' wrote W.A. Darlington in the *Daily Telegraph*. 'It is this sense of being at home in Mr Grahame's domain, of being able to walk in it without watching his step and to talk in it without having to keep a guard on his tongue that has enabled Mr Milne to make such a delightful play.'

But Alan was relieved when Grahame himself came to see the play with his wife, and loved it:

It was almost as if he were thanking me in his royally courteous manner for letting him into the play at all, whereas, of course, it was his play entirely, and all I hoped to do was not to spoil it, he said. For, when characters have been created as solidly as those of Rat and Mole, Toad and Badger, they speak ever after in their own voices, and the dramatist has merely to listen and record.

Alan showed Grahame how much he considered the play to still be his work by taking a much smaller share of the film rights when they were negotiated later, but its success provoked mixed feelings, as Alan had to wonder if perhaps he could only really write well for children, which was the very last thing he wanted.

All four *Winnie-the-Pooh* books continued to sell in huge numbers every year, boosted even further by the first signs of what would eventually mushroom into a vast empire of spin-off merchandising. First came selections from the stories called *Tales of Pooh*, followed by *The Hums of Pooh*, a songbook. *The Christopher Robin Birthday Book* was a compilation of quotations, and then came the *Very Young Calendar*, followed by the *Pooh Calendar*. By the early 1930s there were also birthday cards, Christmas cards, games, toys, and china.

As for Christopher, he and Alan were spending more time together than ever before now they no longer had a nanny, and they were often found solving maths equations or sharing *The Times* crossword. Alan also taught his son the Morse code he had learnt during the war, and relished the hours when it was just the two of them. But those days were not to last. It was around that time that the extent of his fame truly dawned on Christopher, when his riding instructor made what he found a rather confusing remark: 'You see I've got to take care of you,' he told Christopher. 'After all, you're quite an important little personage.'

It was increasingly difficult to protect Christopher from the spotlight. For a long time he had believed his father's stories were written just for him: 'If the books were also being read and enjoyed by complete strangers in Edinburgh and New York, this was something I knew nothing about,' Christopher said. Gradually the outside world was seeping in, he received letters from other children, and the press would turn up at his school – one particularly dogged reporter even disguised herself as a nanny to join the spectators at Macpherson's gymnasium where Christopher took exercise classes. Alan knew all of this, but remained blissfully unaware of how much Christopher was coming to resent his widespread fame. He had not yet blamed his father entirely but as he said himself: 'Christopher Robin was beginning to be what he was later to become, a sore place that looked as if it would never heal up.'

He was falling out of love with the literary version of himself:

It was now that began the love-hate relationship with my fictional namesake that has continued to this day, Christopher said. *At home I still liked him, and indeed felt at times quite proud that I shared his name and was able to bask in some of his glory. At school, however, I began to dislike him, and I found myself disliking him more the older I got. Was my father aware of this? I don't know. Certainly this must have been an anxious period for him. Up to now my mother had been mainly responsible for me. Now it was his turn. He had made me a name, more of a name than he had really intended.*

Although there were moments of discord, during his teenage years Christopher remained largely devoted to his father, and said:

He was lucky. We were together until I was eighteen, very, very close. He knew he was lucky, that he had got perhaps more than he deserved, and he was very grateful. And once, a little shyly, he thanked me.

We had to be on the same level, but we both had to be standing, for my father couldn't bend, couldn't pretend to be what he wasn't. We could do algebra together, and Euclid, and look for birds' nests, and catch things in the stream, and play cricket in the meadow. We could putt on the lawn and throw tennis balls at each other. We could do those things as equals. But what about those other moments, which adults pass in casual chit-chat, which husband and wife can so happily share in complete silence, content to be in each other's company?

Meal times. Car journeys. After dinner in front of the fire. Conversation with a small child is difficult.

We would play clumps, or go through the alphabet to see how many flowers we could name beginning with each letter in turn. And finally, after dinner, almost a ritual, there was The Times crossword with my mother (to give her a slight advantage) reading out the clues and my father trying not to be too quick with the answers.

Christopher's enduring fondness for the work of the Greek philosopher Euclid developed from what he learnt at home, rather than at school, and was a source of great pride to Alan, who boasted about it in a speech he gave to a dinner party of preparatory schoolmasters:

I had disclaimed any desire to make a speech, but this time I wanted to, Alan said. That very evening, offered the alternatives of a proposition of Euclid's or a chapter of Treasure Island as a bedtime story, my own boy had chosen Euclid: it was "so much more fun". All children, I said (perhaps rashly) are like that. There is nothing that they are not eager to learn. And then we send them to your schools, and in two years, three years, four years, you have killed their enthusiasm. At fifteen their only eagerness is to escape learning anything.

Daphne was almost entirely excluded from Alan and Christopher's joint activities and rituals, and she found many of her husband's habits and foibles annoying:

It was generally agreed within the family that my father couldn't eat a pear without getting his elbows wet, and that after a honey sandwich he had to have a bath, Christopher wrote. *There was something cat like about the way my mother ate. Just as a cat will lick at a saucer on and on until not even the ghost of a smell remains, so would my mother scrape at her plate, not greedily, just methodically, until it was spotless. My father, on the other hand, mushed his food up and then left all the bits he didn't like – the gristly bits, the stringy bits, the skinny bits – round the edge. And because they were so different, each found the other's habits mildly irritating. "I wonder why you always have to mash up your strawberries in that rather repellent way."*

And although she was very house proud and constantly redecorating, Daphne was so aggravated by her husband at this stage that she pointedly refused to have his favourite armchair reupholstered: 'Well, I really don't see that there's much point,' she told Alan. 'You could only go and fidget another hole.'

While Daphne forged her own independent life, there was nobody to point out to Alan how uncomfortable the attention made Christopher. He was photographed alongside his father as a teenager, and looking back on those pictures he gave what must be the most damning description:

Alan is different. Alan is difficult. But Alan doesn't wear his heart on his sleeve as the others do. Alan's heart is firmly buttoned up inside his jacket and only the merest hint of it can be seen dancing in his eyes, flickering in the corners of his mouth.

My father's heart remained buttoned up all through his life, and I wouldn't want now to attempt to unbutton it,

There was further heartache in store for Alan when his own father's health began to fail. He tried to remain upbeat about it, and in the last surviving letter to John, Alan filled him in about his work, Christopher's progress at school and his niece's recent wedding. He was concerned about his father's plans to leave large sums of money to Barry, and not his wife Connie:

I have just finished the pencil draft of my second play since the end of February – and am now writing it out properly in ink. I feel very play-ful just now; but I wish one could get plays

Sepia portrait of A.A.Milne, Christopher Robin on his lap, with his teddy bear Winnie the Pooh, taken at their Sussex home by photographer Howard Coster in 1926. (Courtesy of National Portrait Gallery, London)

A.A. Milne standing with Christopher Robin, then aged 5, in a portrait by Howard Coster. (Courtesy of National Portrait Gallery, London)

Close up black and white portrait of A.A. Milne in 1926 by Howard Coster. (Courtesy of National Portrait Gallery, London)

A.A. Milne reclining at home in Sussex with his pipe by Howard Coster. (Courtesy of National Portrait Gallery, London)

A.A. Milne sitting behind Christopher Robin in 1926 by Howard Coster. (Courtesy of National Portrait Gallery, London)

Portrait of *Winnie-the-Pooh* illustrator E.H. Shepard, taken by Howard Coster in 1932. (Courtesy of National Portrait Gallery, London)

A.A. Milne's original application to join The Garrick Club – he dined there most days, and left a huge share of his royalties to the private London gentlemen's club when he died. (Author's Collection)

Cotchford Farm, the Milne family home in Hartfield, Sussex. (Author's Collection)

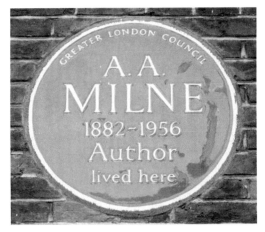

Blue Plaque commemorating A.A. Milne in Mallord Street, Chelsea, the house where Christopher Robin was born. (Author's Collection)

Piglet's House, a tiny door still hidden in a treetrunk in Ashdown Forest. (Author's Collection)

Memorial to A.A. Milne and E.H. Shepard in Ashdown Forest, the inspiration for the Hundred Acre Wood. (Author's Collection)

Pooh Bridge, the famous wooden bridge in Hartfield, Sussex, where Pooh, Piglet and Christopher Robin invented the game of Poohsticks. (Author's Collection)

Sign post indicating the popular Pooh tourist trail through Ashdown Forest and the forest of Hartfield. (Author's Collection)

Embankment Gardens in London, the apartment where Alan and Daphne Milne lived when they were first married. (Author's Collection)

Mr Pim Passes By in 1921.

Christopher Robin's original toys on display at New York Public Library. (Public Domain)

Harry Colebourne and the real Winnie in 1914, source Manitoba Provincial Archives. (Public Domain)

produced as one gets novels published – automatically as soon as the thing is finished. To find in the same person the actor or manager you want and the actor or manager who wants you is always a difficulty.

Moon rides every morning very happily, and amuses himself (and us) in a hundred other ways for the rest of the day. He has grown physically and mentally a lot this term, but hasn't grown away from us, and all the things he loves here, in the least. His bowling has improved a lot, I'm glad to say, and his throwing, and he ought to be certain of getting in the XI this term. He is now 12th in the school (in work) and will be 5th (at least) in September.

I don't want to interfere, but I should suggest that if you altering your will for Connie's sake, you should leave the money definitely to her, not to Barry.

I expect Maud has told you all about the wedding. Marjorie looked very well and happy. I have just had a postcard from Venice saying that marriage has surpassed all her expectations and the sun is shining and everything is delightful. I wish the sun would shine here.

John had not been well enough to attend Ken's daughter's wedding in the Henry VII chapel at Westminster Abbey. She married T.M. Murray-Rust, a master at Westminster School where she had been working for some time as the secretary to the bursar. Alan happily stood in for Ken on the day, and gave away the girl he had written about so often in *Punch* magazine twenty years earlier.

Alan and Ken had joked together about their father's lengthy monologues, which John referred to as his 'talks about things', but Alan always adored him and often talked of how much he owed him. John was incredibly proud of Alan's huge achievements and boasted about his famous son to his friends. But Alan felt guilty when he thought of his father in his later years, eating meals alone at home in Purley, and paid tribute to him in the play *Michael and Mary* when the character of Michael said to his father: 'I do honour you, father. There's something about sheer goodness that always gets me.

Sometimes you irritate me intensely and yet I believe I love you.'

Alan feared that Barry was trying to persuade their father to alter his will from the version he had drawn up after Ken's death three years earlier. In the original will, he planned to return £5,000 which Alan had given his father to help out in his later years, and intended to leave the rest of his estate to Ken's daughters Marjorie and Angela. Alan certainly did not need the money, although he was determined to fulfil his promise that Ken's children were always well provided for.

Barry got solicitors to draw up new documents however, making himself and his own son executors and trustees of the altered will. A few details of John's legacy stayed the same – Ken's two sons would both receive valuable gifts from their grandfather. Tim was to still receive a gold watch and chain, and Tony would inherit 'the clock in the Sitting Room and the framed photograph of Ditchling Pond'. Alan would have 'the walking stick given to me by my wife', and to Daphne he left 'the framed photograph of Christopher Robin Milne and the Venetian Glass on the mantelpiece in the Sitting Room'.

But the rest of the will was completely changed without consulting Alan. There was no mention in the new documents about returning his £5,000, and Angela received only £100. Marjorie meanwhile, who had been extremely close to her grandfather and in constant contact with him, would receive nothing at all.

The rest of John's large and valuable estate was signed over to Barry. John apparently wrote:

All the real and personal property except property otherwise disposed of by this will, I devise and bequeath unto my son David Barrett Milne for his own use and benefit absolutely,'

If John's last wish had been to safeguard Connie's future, as Alan's letter suggested, he had failed entirely. Barry achieved his aim of getting his hands on John's entire fortune, although his attempts to prevent Ken's widow Maud from seeing her dying father-in-law were not so successful. During one of her final visits, John said to her: 'I am sorry about the will.'

CHAPTER EIGHT

It later emerged that Barry had convinced the frail and elderly John that Marjorie's new husband, the Westminster schoolmaster, was extremely rich and could easily take care of her sister Angela too if necessary. John seemed unaware of how little schoolmasters actually earned, and that the newlyweds were living in a modest cottage on the outskirts of London.

Alan could not bear the idea of contesting the will when he heard about the changes, but he vowed to have nothing more to do with his brother from that moment on. He was furious that his beloved nieces had been cheated out of their inheritance by an unscrupulous and greedy uncle. He and Barry had never been particularly close, even in childhood, but now they were out of each other's lives forever. Alan was never able to forgive Barry, and six years later in a letter to his former teacher H.G. Wells he revealed how Barry's son John was trying desperately to leave his father's office: 'He hates it like hell,' Alan wrote. 'And is trying to escape into something, as he thinks, more respectable, like publishing.' His nephew, whom Alan had called Jock in a verse when he was a little boy, eventually left and became an Anglican clergyman. Alan went on: 'In confidence may I say that (for what I think are very good reasons) I have not been on speaking terms with Barry for some years, and see nothing of his family: it is Ken's family which command my interest and cheque book.' Alan would never speak to Barry again, even when he was dying of throat cancer and wrote to his youngest brother begging for a reconciliation.

When John passed away on 11 June 1932, Alan felt as if he had severed every last tie with his childhood. He was 50 years old and for the first time he was neither optimistic nor enthusiastic about the future.

CHAPTER NINE

'You can't stay in your corner of the Forest waiting for others to come to you. ou have to go to them sometimes.'

Alan was absolutely delighted when a customs officer in New York harbour recognised him the first time he docked on American soil in October 1931: 'Can you imagine an English customs man who had read the works of an American author?' he wondered. 'Why, most of them do not read books by Englishmen.' His name was everywhere as sales of the *Winnie-the-Pooh* books had soared to over a million copies in the United States, breaking all previous publishing records.

But his joyful mood was to prove short-lived. Alan was immediately inundated with questions from dozens of reporters, as well as requests for appearances and articles, and suddenly decided that he did not want to give any speeches and would not write anything about the country either. Interviewers were surprised at how difficult they found him, giving only the briefest answers possible to their questions, preferring to sit quietly in the library of the *Aquitania* cruise ship he had sailed in on, smoking his pipe. He argued that he was only visiting America for 'pleasure' although he was in fact there for the opening of his play *They Don't Mean Any Harm*, which had been called *Other People's Lives* when it was performed in Britain.

Alan had desperately hoped this play would be different enough to distance him once and for all from the dreaded word 'whimsical' which he had come to so despise. But there was no escaping it. A review in *Theatre* magazine said: 'For the most part engrossing and delightful, although perhaps overly whimsical for a play built on ideas.' And Joseph Wood Krutch in *The Nation* wrote: 'One short dramatic scene in this sentimental comedy drama is surrounded with padding which may be judged whimsical or infantile.' Alan made his feelings abundantly clear, and they were summed up by a headline in the *New York Tribune*, which blared on his arrival: 'A.A. Milne Here Loathing Name Of "Whimsical". Author of Winnie-the-Pooh Hates Whiskey, Fears Interviewers, will not lecture. Never In America Before. Christopher Robin, Now 11, Remained At Home In School.'

Interviewers said he complained of 'professional jealousy' when asked about his extraordinary book sales, and tried to avoid talking about *Pooh* at all: 'I always like my last book best but I find it's impossible to get away from the "Christopher Robin" atmosphere,' he said. 'When my new novel *Two People* was reviewed in London, all of the critics harped on the same string.' Despite his moans, *Two People* became a best seller in America too, and received glowing reviews, although most readers admitted they only bought the novel because they were interested in seeing what Christopher Robin's father was up to now. Sales were also boosted by a glowing review from his old friend P.G. Wodehouse, who was among the few who no longer saw Alan just as a children's writer. Wodehouse wrote in a letter to a friend from his Hollywood home: 'Have you read A.A. Milne's serial *Two People* in the *Daily Mail*? It's colossal. The sort of book I shall buy and re-read every six months or so. What a genius he is at drawing a character. Did you ever see his *Dover Road*? My favourite play.' More than twenty years later, Wodehouse would write another letter, saying: 'Any news of AAM? You know he did write some damn good stuff. I can re-read a thing like *Two People* over and over again and never get tired of it.'

But apart from Wodehouse, there seemed very few people capable of thinking of Alan as anything other than the *Pooh* author, which he found particularly irritating at this point in his career as he was increasingly desperate to change perceptions. Only a year earlier *Michael and Mary* had enjoyed a hugely successful run in New York, followed by a lucrative tour of major American cities – despite some rather mixed reviews. He was particularly hurt by an attack from the critic George Jean Nathan who said:

I am told that, in his personal being, this Milne is an entirely normal fellow who eats meat, shaves and cusses at a tight cork, just like any of us, but the moment he gets out his writing tools something very peculiar happens to him. He can't check himself from going pansy with a vengeance.

Nathan was among the audiences who were scandalised by an on-stage kiss between a male character and his father.

Yet, despite the fact that thousands of people were buying tickets and filling theatres every night, Alan's adult plays were still not what the press were interested in during that trip to America. All they wanted to hear about was Christopher Robin, and how he was growing up. Fanny Butcher of the *Chicago Tribune* told him: 'Christopher Robin was our chief concern. There's your next novel. The story of Christopher Robin at the age of twenty-two, when he reaps the harvest of his childhood.' Alan replied: 'If I make a success of Christopher Robin as a person I will consider it my greatest creative work.'

In another revealing interview for the *New York Times*, under the headline 'Milne's Hardest Job Is Being A Father,' Alan admitted: 'It is difficult to guide a boy, to direct him in certain channels and at the same time to make him retain the feeling that you are his companion and that there is no separation caused by the gulf of years.' Alan softened a little and shared a few photos of Christopher who was by then 11 years old, and looking far more grown up than when the public last saw him in Shepard's drawings. Clearly he could not 'stay six for ever and ever', as suggested in the poems. Alan cheerfully boasted about his son's impressive skills as a cricket player, and that he had written his first piece of prose called, rather surprisingly, *The Inexperienced Husband*.

Daphne was also required to conduct a series of interviews, usually alongside her husband, while some reporters preferred to speak to her alone. They were thrilled that she was much more prepared to talk about *Pooh*: 'Pooh sheds a tear occasionally when he remembers that he and Christopher Robin were exactly the same size on that day, ten years ago now, when the friendly bear joined the Milne family,' she said. While Christopher Robin was undoubtedly growing up, Daphne did not think he was as mature as his American counterparts:

He is younger I find, than most American children of his age,

CHAPTER NINE

she said. English children seem to belong longer to the nursery than their American cousins. They are less sophisticated, quite babyish really in comparison. Inhabiting a little world all their own, it is not surprising that English children stay very simple and young. Over here life seems to throw American children into closer contact with the older members of the family.

The first time they visited New York Alan and Daphne had both been fascinated with the place. They stayed at what soon became her favourite hotel, the exclusive Lombardy on East Fifty-Sixth Street, and Alan would regularly take himself off exploring the Upper West Side neighbourhood: 'He loves the streets of New York already and you can't keep him in,' noted one interviewer. He was curious about the city, but he also wanted to escape the constant telephone calls and queues of journalists jostling to ask him the same repetitive questions over and over again, and he frequently slipped off for days to the golf courses in the suburbs of Westchester and Long Island.

Daphne said she found New York: 'Much more beautiful, much more interesting and much more delightful' than either of them had expected. She longed to go to a speakeasy, one of the illicit bars which flouted the city's alcohol ban, but Alan declared himself 'extraordinarily uninterested' in the liquor controversy. One thing they did share was a love of theatre, and they went to see plays together almost every evening, gratified to discover that it was much more a part of daily life than it was for people in London: 'At the average lunch or dinner party, the theatre is the principal topic of conversation,' Alan said. He felt that back in Britain tickets were only bought very occasionally, for a special celebration or treat.

During the trip there were many celebrations thrown in the Milne's honour, which Daphne enjoyed far more than her husband did. *Parents* magazine held a tea party, at which the editor Alice Dalgleish announced that Alan's poetry: 'Showed a true understanding of children and had brought America and England closer together.' The magazine named Christopher one of the most famous children in the world – alongside Yehudi Menuhin, Crown Prince Michael of Romania, Princess Elizabeth of England and the child film star Jackie Coogan.

Then there was another, much larger tea party at the Waldorf Astoria Hotel, hosted by John Macrae of Duttons, and Alan was horrified to discover as many as 400 people in the room: 'They invited everybody – literary, dramatic and dilettante,' Macrae recalled. 'The guests came in droves and each had his blunderbuss loaded with a question which he let fly the moment he held Mr Milne's right hand. Meeting people in droves is not Mr Milne's long suit.' Among the distinguished guests lining up to meet Alan that afternoon were Mrs Franklin D. Roosevelt, the British Consul-General, Walter Lippman, Norman Thomas, Fannie Hurst and Christopher Morley – who Dorothy Parker had pretended to confuse with Christopher Robin in her damning review of *Now We Are Six*.

The invitations flooded in thick and fast, and Daphne had trouble keeping up with them all. Despite her best efforts, she was not very organised and inadvertently agreed to a number of social engagements for dates that they were not actually going to be in New York at all, forcing Alan to issue various apologies: 'We go to Philadelphia on Monday and then to Toronto for a day or two,' he explained to the literary critic May Lamberton Becker. 'Do forgive us, and realise how difficult it is for us to keep our heads in this avalanche of hospitality which has descended on us.' He was also anxious about the mixed reception that met the first night of his play. Alan felt it was the most interesting and challenging of all his adult writing so far, telling the story of two couples, the Waites and the Bellamys, who decide to amuse themselves by interfering in the lives of the Tillings, a sad family living in the flat below. *They Don't Mean Any Harm* had an unhappy ending, and some critics thought that it was flawed by tragic implications and 'Ibsenish irony'. *The Saturday Review* slammed it as 'a savage attack on the new generation,' adding 'a nearly great play is disappointing.' Some theatre critics suggested that the nature of the play proved that Alan had at last achieved the adult status he had craved, but *Theatre Arts Monthly* seemed to sum up the more popular opinion with: 'Milne continues his sentimental decline.'

It was a flop, running for only fifteen performances on Broadway, and was the last of Alan's plays to be produced there. Devastated by the disastrous reception, he retreated back to Cotchford to lick his wounds. Struggling with his next novel *Four Days Wonder*, he wrote a miserable letter to his agent, using his cable address which was Chopkins:

Entirely blasted by the shattering disruption of the Chopkins legend, I sat down before the one written chapter of my novel and reflected gloomily that two years would elapse before I rose like a Phoenix from the dust, and faced the world again with a smile, and wreathed vine leaves in my hair.

No I'm damned if I sit down under a failure like that. I will write another and, if not a better play, at least a happier one. Well the whole point of this letter is that I have written two acts of it, and am on my way through the third. It is the lightest Belinda, Hay Fever, Importance of Being Earnest thing, and if it isn't funny I will eat Chopkin's Stetson.

But, unfortunately for Alan, the end result was not funny – or not funny enough – and nobody wanted to produce it. An older play, *The Truth About Blayds*, was revived that April but the critics were no less harsh. One wrote: 'It brought back memories of days when A.A. Milne was a rather exciting figure in the theatre.' And in the *New York Times*, Brooks Atkinson wrote: 'By indulging himself in whimsy, Mr Milne has thrown away a strong career.' Another hammered the final nail in Alan's playwriting career by saying: 'Milne blamed *Pooh* for overshadowing his later plays. But *Pooh* was blameless. Throughout the 1930s Milne produced nothing to overshadow.'

There can be no doubt that a career which had meant so much to Alan, that of a playwright, was brought to a depressing and juddering halt at this point. And yet he refused to accept that it was over, and tried his best to remain fairly optimistic and buoyant, continuing to produce a stream of scripts that would never be staged. Among them were *H for Helena: A Midsummer Night's Folly,* which survives only in his original manuscript; and *Sarah Simple*, which Leonora Corbett would eventually star in when it was produced in London very briefly five years later.

CHAPTER TEN

'A day without a friend is like a pot without a single drop of honey left inside.'

Rather than sitting back and congratulating himself on the phenomenal success of *Winnie-The-Pooh*, Alan ploughed on, still struggling to accept that he could not repeat the same achievements with adult literature, and continued to write at a frantic rate. His output was prolific; he managed to publish six more books in the next five years. One was the novel *Four Days Wonder*, published in 1933, and four were single plays or collections of plays that he had already written. Only one, a political analysis called *Peace With Honour*, would make any significant difference to his reputation.

Any spare time would be spent with Christopher, or as he put it in a letter to his niece: 'Acting as private chauffeur (unpaid) to my boy, who has been playing cricket matches all over Sussex.' But Alan felt he was becoming lazy, claiming: 'I'm a born slacker really.' He had a puritanical streak, and a strong work ethic instilled in him by his hard-working father, which made it almost impossible for him to enjoy an entire day in the garden, or a leisurely round of golf, unless he had some work in progress at the same time. And even when he did manage to sit still, he could usually find something to complain about, and as the summer of 1933 wore on, it was the abundance of horseflies plaguing his garden: 'They definitely like me, even if the critics don't,' he moaned.

In September, Christopher left for his first term at Stowe, where he immediately dropped the name of Robin in a bid to blend in. With more time on his hands, Alan attempted a return to his first love, sketches for *Punch* magazine. He wrote a piece about a prep school boy called John, the name Alan had previously used for Ken in his writing. This lightly disguised version of Christopher was also a good cricketer, and had 'a pleasant touch on the ukulele' – an instrument which Christopher also played well, to the dismay of the music master when he arrived at Stowe. It was the first article Alan had submitted to *Punch* for many years, and he decided to use the pseudonym C.P. Brice. First he sent the manuscript to Marjorie, asking her or her sister Angela to type it up for him in case anybody recognised his distinctive handwriting. He also attached a heartfelt letter boasting about Christopher's cricketing achievements, and congratulating her husband on becoming a housemaster at Westminster, meaning the couple would be based much closer to him at the school from that term onwards. Alan was delighted as he could see much more of them than when they lived in Walthamstow:

> *I am terribly glad and do congratulate you, he wrote. Moon came back last Thursday and we had two heavenly days at Lords. You never saw such batting! We hugged each other in ecstasy at Walters: the most lovely bat in the world.*
>
> *Will you be an angel or get Angela to be one? Egged on by the family I have written the enclosed (obviously from life) and am sending it to Punch anonymously. Could you – would you – type it for me? My handwriting might be recognised. It's not to be A.A.M. in any case, and I thought it would be fun to see if Punch encourages the unknown beginner, and Daff thought it would be fun to send it in as from 'C. Brice' and pinch the money. And her writing is not quite manly enough.*

To Alan's great disappointment, his experiment failed, *Punch* did not encourage the unknown beginner. Without a well-known name attached to it, the magazine had no interest in publishing the piece and it was swiftly returned. Alan was annoyed: 'What the hell?' he asked Marjorie. He sent it back again, this time under his real name, and it was immediately accepted. While he was disheartened to discover that his writing was not appreciated on its own merits, Alan was cheered up immensely by discovering, while dining with Marjorie one evening, that the boys at Westminster School were preparing a production of his first play *Wurzel-Flummery*. He slipped in to watch the rehearsals unnoticed and was thrilled to see the boys laughing in all the right places. He returned for the performance, and sat among scores of parents, telling them later how pleased he was that the play had survived, even if privately he felt that his reputation was in tatters.

And Christopher was not much happier either. He had originally been due to go to Harrow School, and won a scholarship, but was relieved when his parents agreed to turn it down and send him to Stowe instead, which he felt sure would be a much more suitable alternative given his personality:

> *I was shy, solitary, awkward in company, inarticulate in speech, becoming worse as I grew older,* Christopher explained. *How lucky, then, I was to have parents who understood, who felt that, though perhaps what I needed for my own ultimate good was to be thrown in at the deep end, this was where, happily or otherwise, I was spending my term-time, so that during the holidays it was only kind to allow me to enjoy myself in the shallows.*

Christopher sang in the choir and was fairly sporty, but his stutter meant he was not good on the telephone, so whenever it was his turn to arrange teams for cricket matches, Alan would step in, glad of a reason to be useful. With Christopher away during term time, he had too much time on his hands. Daphne was making more and more frequent visits to her lover in New York, and on the night Alan that was among the audience of *Wurzel-Flummery* at Westminster, Daphne was already enjoying her eighth visit. But far from objecting or even appearing to mind, Alan made sure she had plenty of money to enjoy herself. When they had travelled there together and he signed a contract with Dutton for *The Christopher Robin Verses*, two new books in one volume, he asked that they should hold on to $750 of his advance 'for the use of Mrs Milne' when she next returned to America.

While she was away, Alan tended to avoid socialising, preferring quiet dinners with his nieces. Angela was following in her uncle's footsteps and becoming a writer, and he was delighted to have the chance to nurture her ambition, helping her land her first job on the *Evening News*, and later she started to write regularly for *Punch*. She always enjoyed their meals together at some of his favourite haunts including Coq d'Or, the Berkeley and Luigi's in St James's where Alan always ordered the haddock omelettes a la Arnold Bennett. Angela later described her beloved uncle as 'a radiant being'. Very occasionally he entertained at home, and maintained a long-standing friendship with novelist Denis Mackail and his wife Diana, who he sometimes invited to join him for dinner or at the theatre.

Christopher explained that his father turned down scores of party invitations for fear of being thought of as a show off. But other people would remember him quite differently. H.F. Ellis, a writer who joined *Punch* in 1931, was excited when he had the opportunity of meeting Alan, who was among his literary heroes, at a mutual friend's cocktail party:

I was then a very new addition to the editorial staff, and was greatly thrilled when somebody said, "That's Alan Milne over there," because in my day he and Knox and Herbert had formed a kind of Pantheon of humorous writers in my mind. Milne's characters, Myra and Thomas and Simpson, all those Rabbits, had seemed to a teenager just the sort of attractive people one would like to meet. And to meet their creator, well! What hilarious witticism would greet me, when I was introduced? Was it even possible that the great man would say he had enjoyed my last week's article? What he actually said was "Have you managed to get hold of a drink? I haven't." That was the sum total of our conversation.

When Alan's novel *Four Days' Wonder* was published in October 1933, he dedicated it to his old friend from *Punch*, Edward Lucas, who had been promoted to chairman of Methuen: 'To E.V. Lucas whose company now officially an honour has always been a delight,' he wrote. But in spite of the friendly dedication Alan was annoyed that his publishing house had not done as much as they could have to promote him as a writer for adults, and Lucas received an angry letter expressing his bitterness:

I know that Publishers get as annoyed by the importunities of Authors as Schoolmasters by the importunities of Parents. And probably rightly. But I also know that there has never been a less importunate author (or, for that matter, parent) than myself. So now I shall indulge myself and ask: Cannot you make a bit of a fuss of Four Days' Wonder in the way that every other publisher does for his best-selling author? In The Observer last Sunday, there were great thick slabs of space taken for practically every book published at the same time as mine – half a column for Trumpeter, Sound! – and not even the usual inch in a long list of other books (which is Methuen's idea of letting themselves go) for F.D.W.

Why cannot Methuen occasionally have picturesque, eye-catching advertisements of single books, as every other publisher does? What is there about Methuen advertisements (when there) which make their books seem so damn dull?

Now I entreat you to spread yourselves on an advertisement of F.D.W. by itself with some or all of the enclosed extracts from the reviews. I hate pushing myself on you like this, but I really think the firm owes me something, and to be perfectly candid my dear E.V., I cannot feel that it has done anything for me yet.

The letter clearly had the desired effect as a flurry of publicity appeared in the newspapers a few days later, which Alan was shown by his friends at Ashdown Golf Club: 'The advertisement was much appreciated in the Forest country,' he wrote. 'Many thanks.' It was a relief to Alan who always found it difficult trying to interest his neighbours in his writing. His niece Angela once told how Alan took her to visit a Colonel who was living nearby, 'as visitors to East Africa might be driven out to see a giraffe,' she recalled. Their lack of enthusiasm annoyed Alan enormously, especially since he had never had the slightest trouble getting people to buy the children's books; on the contrary, they were always asking for signed copies and when he planned to write more. The sales of the *Winnie-the-Pooh* books showed no signs of slackening off, with a constant supply children being born who needed presents. The popularity never even waned slightly, and it was not just in America and Britain that people adored them. During the 1930s the books were translated into a number of different languages, and many more would follow after the war.

The characters were growing more and more familiar by the day, and in 1933 Alan's bumper royalty cheque from Curtis Brown included a fat slice of the profits from phenomenal sales of soft toys, jigsaw puzzles, modelling sets, and board games. But no matter how much Alan protested, the adult books were a different matter entirely. He had such high hopes for *Four Days' Wonder*, but sales never came close, despite a glowing review in the *Times Literary Supplement*, which said: 'An entirely delightful and brilliant novel. Elegant and gay – it is all capital fun.' Other reviews were not quite so sympathetic, complaining about the implausibility of the plot line involving a rather silly woman called Jenny who runs away to avoid being accused of her aunt's accidental death. When the novel was released in New York, Alan fumed again because his publisher at Dutton's had also failed to market it properly: 'I hear that Macrae has entirely ruined the book by publishing it as my 'latest mystery story' with a corpse on the cover. Hell. Why don't people learn to read?'

His fans clamoured for more children's stories, or a return to the comedy sketches which had been so popular in *Punch* in the past. Harold Raymond from the publishing house Chatto and Windus wrote to Alan, urging him: 'What the world is waiting for, and that is a humorous novel. That particular field is a gaping void. I would give much to laugh again as I used to with your Rabbits, which I can still quote in chunks.'

Although *Four Days' Wonder* sold poorly compared to the children's books, it could still be considered a success overall. It sold

8,000 copies by the end of 1933, and was translated into French, Hungarian and German, but Alan was disappointed and it would be another thirteen years before he published another novel, in 1946. Instead he took to firing off bitter responses to reviewers who he felt did not take his work seriously enough. When Graham Greene, who had just published his novel *Stamboul Train*, reviewed Alan's book for *The Spectator* he called it 'peculiarly dismal'. Greene wrote:

In recommending a novel as funny, one is haunted by a number of long faces registering disapproval or a complete inability to see the joke. The reviewer, to avoid disappointing those whose taste in humour is not his own, should perhaps try to explain once and for all what he considers funny and why.

On what general law is the taste formed of those who, like himself, find the novels, poems or articles of Mr A.A. Milne, of Mr J.B. Morton, of Mr A.P. Herbert, of Mr Denis Mackail, or almost any of the contributors to Punch peculiarly dismal, while they enjoy the works of Mr Peter Arno, of the authors of Is Sex Necessary? And of Miss Yvonne Cloud?

There is one obvious difference between these two groups: Mr Milne's group is on the side of the big battalions. A French psychologist has said that laughter is "l'expression de l'individualite" but these writers are the cheer-leaders in a great community laugh. All these writers have the same attitude to themselves. It is obvious in their work that they have clean minds, a refinement of the popular taste of the time, and that they believe (how they believe it!) that they are right. Their rectitude is fatal to their humour, for if to be right means anything in their case at all, it means the acceptance of the prevailing social codes, from which it should be the function of humour temporarily to release us.

The inferior humourist flatters his public; he laughs with them at what they do not understand, thus easing their distrust, but the material for this kind of humorous changes with every generation.

CHAPTER TEN

Alan was absolutely incensed by this article, and fired back a long letter to the editor, explaining how much he hated being labelled as someone who accepts 'the prevailing social codes'. He wrote:

Mr Greene's sense of humour is his own. Nobody is going to quarrel with him about it, least of all the author who does not amuse him. But when he sets out to "explain once and for all what he considers funny and why" he simply cannot be allowed to get away with it. For at any moment he may try to explain something else. It becomes a public duty, therefore, to which I sacrifice myself not unwillingly "once and for all" to expose his methods.

Mr Greene dislikes four writers – Mackail, Herbert, Morton and Milne – who have nothing in common but the fact that he dislikes them. Having called them "Mr Milne's group", he is then in a position to identify them all with Punch. Milne himself resigned from Punch fifteen years ago; about the time when Mr Churchill, that ardent Liberal, resigned from the Liberal Party. Mackail has never written for Punch. Morton not only has never written for Punch, but is definitely (and I fancy, vociferously) antagonistic to it. This leaves only Herbert, the one Punch survivor; a writer whose contributions to Punch are quite notably out of alignment with the rest of the paper. No matter to Mr Greene. All his fierce reaction against Punch (which in some odd way he seems to hold responsible for his sex-repressions) can now be transferred to the Milne Group. The Wicked Four are "on the side of the big battalions;" they accept "the prevailing social codes from which it should be the function of humour temporarily to release us"; they are "the cheer-leaders in a great community laugh."

All through Mr Greene's article one gets this sense of special pleading and superficial thinking. He never seems to follow his thoughts to any length. If the only stable humour were the humour that shocks, then the capacity of receiving a shock would have to be a stable; which notoriously it isn't.

When the controversy was reported, Alan came across badly and critics feared he had lost his famous sense of humour. *Living Age* magazine in America suggested: 'Mr Milne is never quite so dull as when he tries to defend his rights as a humourist.' But he was as tired of being branded a humourist as he was of being dismissed as a whimsical children's storyteller. What annoyed him most was the fact that the *Pooh* books only amounted to a total of less than a hundred thousands words of his vast back catalogue, and yet they were all that anyone wanted to read:

> *It is easier in England to make a reputation than to lose one, he said. I wrote four children's books, containing altogether, I suppose 70,000 words – the number of words in the average length novel. Having said goodbye to all that in 70,000 words, knowing that as far as I was concerned the mode was outdated, I gave up writing children's books. I wanted to escape from them as I had once wanted to escape from Punch; as I have always wanted to escape. In vain. As a discerning critic pointed out: the hero of my latest play, God help it, was 'just Christopher Robin grown up'. So that when I stop writing about children I still insist on writing about people who were children once. What an obsession with me children are become!*

CHAPTER ELEVEN

'If the person you are talking to doesn't appear to be listening, be patient. It may simply be that he has a small piece of fluff in his ear.'

Since Ken's death, Alan had been mulling over a number of ideas and political theories which he eventually wrote in *Peace With Honour*. It was his first academic book, and the one he always considered the most important. When he submitted the manuscript he urged John Macrae at Dutton's to take it seriously: 'You have always told me that personally you thought more of *Winnie-the-Pooh* than of any other book I have ever written. Please let me tell you that I think more of *Peace With Honour* than of any book that I have ever written.' Luckily Macrae agreed with him, and replied: 'I believe that *Peace With Honour* will have the greatest influence of any book in modern times.'

With a second world war looming on the horizon, it was a time of fierce patriotism, but Alan had openly branded himself a pacifist since 1910, and in this book he made a passionate plea for peace and a renunciation of war. His traumatic experiences during the First World War continued to haunt him and inevitably reinforced the strength of his conviction that war was a horrendous, and ineffective, way to solve international disputes. He felt strongly about the subject, but struggled to write without any dialogue or characters to do the talking for him, and it took him years to get to grips with straight prose. 'I have been trying to write it, and in a sense, trying not to write it for the last five years. I have actually written it in the last twelve months between July 1933 and July 1934,' he explained in the book's preface.

He was so completely consumed with the book that he was forced to apologise to publishers Chatto and Windus for not having prepared the script of *Other People's Lives* for publication as agreed. The play had just closed in the West End but Alan's thoughts were elsewhere by then: 'I felt sick of the whole thing and not at all in the mood to grapple with it for the press; in fact, I felt that I never wanted to see the dashed play again,' he wrote. 'Curse the theatre. Curse all plays. No matter – avanti.'

Given the chilling political wind blowing across Europe in 1934, Alan found it increasingly inappropriate to try to be funny. In January that year, at a rally of right wing 'Black Shirts' in Birmingham, ten thousand people heard Sir Oswald Mosley ask Britain to return a fascist majority, and Alan was appalled. He attempted to write a piece of light verse but could not see very much to laugh about. What he saw was a generation of bored young men turning to war games for sport, and it terrified him. With Adolf Hitler leading the Black Shirts' counterparts in Germany, it was not easy to raise a smile, but he tried:

> *O Life was a bore*
> *As we said before,*
> *So we joined the Shirts and we played at War*
> *And now at last our life*
> *Is like a tree that's fruited.*
> *Each night we tell the wife*
> *How often we're saluted.*
> *So fervent is the hail*
> *Our Leader gets on Sunday,*
> *He simply cannot fail*
> *To lead us somewhere one day.*

Like many others, Alan never forgot the inhumanity he witnessed in the Somme, and what he feared most was the outbreak of another war. He became even more gravely concerned when Hitler withdrew Germany from the League of Nations, as he had hoped that the League could encourage the forces for peace to unite, which would be the best chance of overcoming fascism without another war. Alan felt huge sympathy with the young men at the Oxford University Union who voted overwhelmingly in a debate not to 'fight for its King and

Country'. As a passionate supporter of peace, he wrote at length in response to a piece by journalist J.A. Spender who reported the outcome of the university debating club in the *News Chronicle*:

The Oxford motion expresses, not merely the determination not to fight an aggressive war, but the confidence that the youth of other nations is equally determined, he wrote. Fortunately, however, the supporters of the motion meant to vote for more than that. They were putting on record (I think and hope) two convictions:

1. It is impossible to ensure Peace so long as a distinction is drawn between aggressive and defensive war.

In his heart Mr Spender knows this just as well as I do. He knows that never in history has a war been fought without each side claiming that the other was the aggressor. Indeed, one might almost say that no country had ever fought anything but a defensive war. Not only that, but no country has ever fired the first shot.

But there is another reason why Peace can recognise no distinction between attack and defence. It is that you cannot have defence without armaments, and that armaments, as Mr Spender knows, are the deadly enemy of Peace.

2. The one thing that has kept War alive, now that its hideous wickedness and waste has been revealed, is sentimentality.

For England that sentimentality is epitomised in the words "King and Country". You can take – no, let me say that in 1914 you could take any decent, chivalrous, clean-living, God fearing young man, whisper the words "King and Country" in his ear, and send him off in an aeroplane to disembowel women and children, and he would go cheerfully, with the knowledge that he carried with him on his errand the love of his own women and the prayers of his church.

In 1899 you could whisper "King and Country" in the ears of honourable, fair-minded, intelligent men, and set them waving their hats and screaming for a war as undefensible [sic] and unadmirable as the Boer War. There is no infamy for which the words "King and Country" do not provide adequate cover. "My country, right or wrong!" How tragically easy war becomes waged in these mists of sentimentality.

So I rejoice that two hundred and fifty young men have had the courage to say boldly that War is a Crime, that it is a Crime which must be renounced without condition, and that it is not less a crime because "King and Country" demand it. Strange as it may seem to certain people, one can say it and yet love one's country and honour one's King.

And if anyone doubts the urgent need of saying it let him study the response which the "loyal" and "patriotic" have made: the white feathers, the shriek of "Cowards!" There you have the hysterical war-mind, ready to talk good, comfortable, patriotic, conditional peace until the next Armageddon.

Joining forces with several other writers who also spoke out against the idea of war, Alan added: 'I am convinced that every such sort of writing helps to kill the war spirit.' In another letter thanking the politician Lord Ponsonby for a copy of his book *Disarmament*, he wrote: 'I feel both ashamed and proud; ashamed that I had not read it before, and proud that, starting to think out war all over again, I have used exactly your arguments and reached so finally your conclusions. Between us we *must* be right.'

As 1934 drew to a close another war seemed inevitable, given the failure of the 1932 General Disarmament Conference in Geneva and the overt militarism of Japan, Italy, and Germany, which seemed to be changing the general attitude to pacifism that flourished in Britain following the huge losses on the battlefields of northern France in the First World War. As reports began to filter through of Nazi policies sweeping Germany, Alan was more determined than ever to do what he could to save another generation having to endure warfare. He could not bear the idea of Christopher having to join the army. It may have been idealistic, and perhaps ultimately unrealistic, to think he could change millions of people's minds, but Alan felt sure that the world leaders who made terrible decisions while avoiding battle themselves could not ignore him forever: 'If everybody reads the book (which is unlikely) then the thing is done. There is an end of war,' he insisted.

But once again he worried that his usual publishing house Methuen would not do enough to promote the book, as he wanted it pushed not just for the sake of sales but also for political purposes. Writing to E.V. Lucas he admitted that he was considering sending his manuscript to various rival publishers as the managing director Emile Rieu might not be enthusiastic enough for his liking:

> *This is why I lean to some more 'advanced' firm like Gollancz – I mean advanced politically, he said. Methuen may be too respectable. You aren't, thank Heaven, but Rieu is, and he will definitely hate the book, and be very cold and tight mouthed about it. You will like it, I think. Macrae will do it in America. He is just the man for it and will send a copy to every Senator and every clergyman in the country, and let himself go over it. You realise, of course, that my anxiety for enormous sales is the anxiety of a Pacifist, rather than of a tax payer.*

He urged senior officers and generals in the British Army to read his book, and even asked Lucas to send a copy to the King George V: 'He won't read it,' he said. 'But it may do the Dean of Windsor a bit of good.'

A questionnaire in the *Bookman* magazine in 1934 aimed to discover how several eminent writers of the day felt about the political situation. Many buried their heads in the sand when it came to the first heavily loaded question, which asked: 'Can you, as an individual, declare the state of things today, even in our own country, in their totality, humanly tolerable?' While some of his fellow writers said they felt that things were actually better than at any time in the past, Alan replied that the situation in Britain was absolutely unacceptable. All his answers to the questionnaire show how his mind was 'intolerably preoccupied' with world affairs, and that he was only able to relieve the immense pressure by writing. In answer to the question, 'How would you briefly define the relevance of your art to these existing conditions?' he answered: 'All art is witness to the sanctity of the individual and never was such witness wanted as it is today.'

Alan desperately hoped that his book would change people's minds, and make them think like he did. And when it was finally published, he was so relieved by the positive reaction that he felt 'more hopeful at the moment than I ever have before'. The *New York Times* reported that *Peace With Honour* was in greater demand in bookstores than any other non-fiction book apart from H.G. Wells' autobiography. And by the end of the year, just three months after publication, it had already sold an impressive 12,000 copies. Despite the rise of right wing politics, he had tapped into a popular longing for pacifism. But Alan knew that to stand any chance of avoiding war he had to convince the key European leaders who held the real power to take an oath renouncing war: 'I suppose one must assume that Great Statesmen are real people; and go on talking, and writing, in the hope that somehow, sometime, one will make contact,' he said.

Many of his ideals were thought to be unrealistic, and the outcomes he dreamt of were impossible, but *The Times* ran an enthusiastic review under the headline 'The Case Against War. Mr Milne's Brilliant Attack.' 'Mr Milne's tremendous earnestness has not weakened the happiness of his literary touch,' the piece said, agreeing that his book was 'a very serious and able challenge to conventional thought,' but adding: 'Issues can arise which will simply not submit themselves to arbitral decision, even by the most impartial minds, and that those who hold that war cannot be renounced unless it can be prevented have something of a philosophy to back their view.'

An in-depth discussion of the evils of modern war was always bound to fiercely divide critics, and when the historian Basil Liddell Hart reviewed it for *The Daily Telegraph* he argued:

A more irrational way of settling a question than by force is rationally inconceivable. I can never understand why the trite question, "Would you stand by while an enemy raped your mother or sister?" is so popular with those who disbelieve in pacifism. A far more pertinent question would be: "Can you hope to reason with a mad dog?"

Alan's argument was that he was 'absolutely certain that another European war would mean the complete collapse of civilisation'. He would eventually be proved wrong, but Liddell Hart was deeply fascinated by the theory and the two began to correspond regularly following his review. In one letter, Liddell Hart wrote: 'With much that you add I am in agreement but there are certain aspects which I feel might both help to clear out our own minds if we were to thrash out points in discussion, so I suggest that, if you have time, we might lunch together one day.'

The eminent historian was by no means alone in wanting Alan to discuss his subject at more length, and he was invited on a lecture tour across Europe but turned it down because he wanted time to write another novel. He was also asked to speak in dozens of schools and churches and attend numerous Armistice Day ceremonies, but he hated public speaking and refused them all.

One offer he did accept however was to take part in a political debate at the BBC. He wrote to Lucas explaining his surprising decision to take chairman Lord Reith up on his offer:

Damn it, I am doing the last. Not for Reith's bright eyes, or my own, or yours (though it will be dashed good advertisement) but entirely because I have a sick, uneasy feeling that it is my DUTY. Really, there is only one word in the English language which is essential to the conduct of life and that is 'No!' And to say it a mere 23 times out of 24 isn't anything like enough.

His usual way of declining was with a polite: 'Unfortunately this is a thing which I don't do', but Alan was also persuaded to speak on the subject of 'Peace and War' at several major public schools including Uppingham, Marlborough and of course Stowe, giving him an extra excuse to see Christopher: 'A few years ago one couldn't have come within a mile of a public school with a book like this in one's pocket without police protection,' Alan wrote in one of his many letters to best friend Charles Turley Smith, known as Turley. 'Moon tells me that "hundreds" of boys at Stowe have read it.' Christopher was just relieved that his peers had something to distract them from *Winnie-the-Pooh* but Alan was immensely flattered by the invitations to such prominent schools: 'Twenty years ago it wouldn't have been possible without the protection of half a dozen policemen and an emergency Union Jack,' he added. 'A few years ago one would have wanted a false beard. Even schoolmasters are becoming human.'

The most unexpected people agreed with his arguments, among them Queen Marie of Romania, who wrote from Bucharest:

This letter will probably astonish you – I know nothing about you, not even if you are old or young, but I had to write and tell you that I wholeheartedly agree with all you say. I am but a retired queen who has to sit still and contemplate with horror the blind rush towards destruction, which seems to have taken possession of great and small. Here in my faraway corner, I spend hours pondering over what could and should be done, deploring that the strength is not given to me to stand up and cry Stop! Before it is too late; like the prophets of old I would cry out the truth and try to tear the bandage from their eyes, force our leaders to work for peace instead of war, for mutual understanding instead of adding daily to the increasing distrust and paralysing fear of each other.

His postbag also included:

Letters from Communists who insist that we can never get peace until capitalism is abolished from Social Creditors who proclaim that Social Credit is the only way to peace, from Oxford Groupers who maintain that peace cannot come save through the change of heart which Dr Buchman assures his

followers. At any moment I may get a letter from a Flat Earther
warning me that only in a completely flat world can we escape
from war.

Alan tried to respond to as much of the correspondence as he could, reiterating: 'War is, in almost all cases, neither a cure nor prevention of the disease which it seems to treat, but merely a postponement of it.' He even managed to get his anti-war message through to a few members of the army who decided to completely change the course of their lives and careers after reading his book. One such young officer was David Spreckley, who was serving in the Royal Dragoons in India when the book made him question everything he had stood for and believed in up until that point:

I was very lucky since a series of unconnected and fortuitous
happenings had already started my tiny cloistered mind thinking
for itself, he explained. The Establishment, the British Raj, the
Church of England – were they, after all, such a good thing?
Why should I, a spotty (probably) boy of twenty have twenty-
three Indian servants? Yes, twenty-three – one of whose sole
function was the emptying of my 'thunder box' (earth closet).
One day I walked into the library of the Officers' Club and
picked up – unbelievably – Peace With Honour. Don't ask me
how it got there. I read it, then read it straight through again. It
was, so far as my memory goes, very simple stuff – just right for
my mind at the time – and it did the trick. The fragile glass ball
which had cocooned me was shattered. Six months later – to the
great relief of my fellow officers – I resigned my commission. I
wanted more time to think so I rode round England on a horse
for three months, then signed Dick Sheppard's pledge and joined
the staff of the Peace Pledge Union.

The Peace Pledge Union was a British non-governmental pacifist movement, set up by the Canon of St Paul's Cathedral Richard Sheppard, who was horrified by what he had witnessed in military field hospitals. Anyone could join if they took the PPU Pledge: 'I renounce war, and am therefore determined not to support any kind of war, I am also determined to work for the removal of all causes of war.' Within weeks of announcing the initiative, thousands had pledged their support, and the movement is still active today.

In spite of Sheppard's many appeals, Alan did not become a member: 'I don't like pledging myself to anything,' he explained. However, *Peace With Honour* became one of only three books named as recommended reading for members, who were also sent a list of hints to help them be more effective when it came to presenting their political arguments – tips included 'Keep your humour' and 'Be courteous in debate.'

Instead of backing the PPU, Alan put his energy into supporting the League of Nations Union, which he felt sure was the better agency for promoting peace around the globe. He hoped that a more international approach to diplomacy would free England from its attachment to the colonies and what he saw as the country's obsession with becoming a Great Power. He feared that the rest of the world saw the British Empire not as a guarantee of peace but of trouble. He wrote:

When the patriot cries that England's prestige is in danger, he means that England's reputation as a Great Power is in danger; by which he means only this: that England's reputation for war-capacity is in danger.

It is not understandable that the sacro-sanctity of the Empire, and of every line, visible or invisible, connecting up the Empire, does not seem to the foreigner to be the clue to the world's happiness. It would be an advantage if just occasionally we could discard that hypocrisy which, to the foreigner, is so infuriatingly characteristic of England. Of course we want peace. What dictator, once in power, what tyrant, what plutocrat ever wanted civil war?

Alan became so passionate in his campaign to avoid another war that in 1935 he wrote a widely circulated pamphlet for the League of

Nations under the title *Five Minutes of Your Time*, repeating his argument that nobody really wanted war, but hardly anyone in England was prepared to do anything to prevent one breaking out:

> *Now for the first time in the history of the world we are trying a new international law, a new way of thought. And your reason for turning it down is that it hasn't been immediately successful! Why, you might as well have turned down steam engines because Stephenson's first train ran into a cow.*

I suppose it's because I'm British, and don't like the idea of getting mixed up with other nations....

> *You can't help being mixed up with other nations in these days. Any part of Europe is nearer to England today than London was to Liverpool in 1800. The world is a League of Nations whether you like it or not.*

While many supported Alan, he had a formidable opponent in the poet T.S. Eliot who was just finding fame with his new play *Murder in the Cathedral*. The two writers appeared on the surface to have a great deal in common, but it soon became clear that there was a gulf between their social attitudes. Eliot took Alan to task in a piece entitled *Notes on the Way*, which was published in *Time and Tide* magazine in January 1935. He criticised his rival for being 'so devoured by the thought that War is Bad that he cannot see that a great many other things are bad too'. Eliot added:

> *I am not reviewing Milne's book, but only taking it as an instance of what seems to me a frequent type of confused and insufficient thinking about war. And it is appropriate I should consider Mr Milne rather than any of the more professional writers about war, such as Sir Norman Angell, because I take him to be a simple man of letters like myself, with a sense of public responsibility.*

Eliot was referring to the man who had been largely responsible for converting Alan to pacifism twenty-five years earlier, Labour MP Sir Norman Angell had been a prominent member of both the League of Nations Union and the World Committee Against War and Fascism, and was eventually awarded the Nobel Peace Prize.

'I share his feelings about militaristic utterances by foreign statesmen,' Eliot went on. But he did not share Alan's total condemnation of war under any circumstances, and felt he was being naïve and idealistic. Alan insisted that any kind of peace would be preferable to the hell he saw on the Somme.

Eliot concluded: 'The difference here is between those who believe in original sin and those who do not. War is in itself a bad thing, we all agree. But what, as things are, is Peace? Or as things may be?' The newspapers buzzed for weeks with responses to Eliot's article, and Alan's own letter appeared on 19 January:

> *I should not have considered it possible that anybody could read my book and suppose that I regarded Peace as beautiful in itself, or the social system as perfection,* he wrote. *But, no doubt, if I denounced the slums, Mr Eliot would tell us that writers of my type suffered from the prejudice that house-room was a beautiful thing in itself; and would assure us that the only mansion worth having was a mansion in the skies.*
>
> *For his rule of life seems to be that nothing is worth doing unless you can convince yourself that there is nothing better worth doing, and as you can never do this you had better do nothing. He says: "I do not see how you can condemn war in the abstract unless you assert a) that here is no higher value than Peace; b) that there is nothing worth fighting for; and c) that a war in which one side is right and the other is wrong is inconceivable." I am prepared to admit that any number of particular wars have been unjustifiable by either side, but not to admit the foregoing assumptions.*
>
> *I should have supposed that you could a) condemn adultery without asserting that there is no higher value than not living*

*in adultery; b) believe that there are things worth fighting for,
and worth dying for, but worth bombing babies for; and c)
condemn duelling in the abstract without asserting that a duel
in which one side is right and the other wrong is inconceivable.
Mr Eliot, however, will not admit any of these assumptions. He
arrives in his fourth column at the remarkable conclusion:
"War is in itself a bad thing, we all agree." A bad thing, but he
can't condemn it – nor help us make an end of it.*

As the public dispute between the two well-known writers rumbled
on it became increasingly heated, but to his surprise, Alan's point of
view seemed to be gathering the weight of public opinion, which
swung onto his side thanks to Eliot firing off insults including: 'Mr
Milne continues to involve himself, like a cat in fly paper, in
comparisons or analogies which he cannot control. Not knowing that
Mr Milne had begun thinking about war, I did not know that he had
finished.'

Although Eliot would be proved right eventually, since war would
soon break out; much of the country had not recovered from the First
World War and desperately hoped history would not repeat itself. By
voicing what they were thinking, Alan emerged from the encounter
with his reputation very much intact. In a letter to *The Times* he wrote
on behalf of the ordinary man in the street:

*No doubt most of us prefer peace to war. The great men who
have been writing to you all talk of "wanting peace" as if this
were all that is to be said for it. What remains to be said is how
much if anything, a man or a country is prepared to sacrifice
for it. I suggest to the ordinary man that he begins by
sacrificing a little of his time in answering the questions "Yes"
"No" or "See Below" and amplifying his answers. After all,
what else can he do?*

The last question was a highly pertinent one, as most people feared
there was very little they could actually do to prevent the rise of

fascism. Alan was doing all he could, but feared it was not enough. He was among the fervent supporters of a Peace Ballot, a petition to gauge the strength of public opinion, which quickly gathered more than eleven million signatures. But few could imagine the extent of Hitler's ambition and lunacy, Alan certainly could not despite a stark warning from Gilbert Murray, a professor of Greek at Oxford University, who wrote to Alan saying how much he 'loved' the book. Murray pointed out that Alan had failed to take into account the unpredictable actions of lunatics:

> *I have just been looking up a passage in Hitler's Mein Kampf where he explains that the annihilation (Vernichtung) of France is the only one necessary step in the realisation of Germany's proper position. The others, if I understand his rather obscure style, are the removal of all racially impure persons (Slavs, Latins etc.) from Europe, so as to leave it in possession of two hundred and fifty million Germans.*

A few years later the dictator seized power, but Alan remained convinced that Hitler did not stand a chance of putting his plans into action, and replied to Murray: 'As for the insatiable ambitions, has anyone tried satisfying them? How many ambitions could be satisfied for a tenth of the cost of the last war. But, of course, lunatics *are* the difficulty.'

Alan was also becoming increasingly disturbed by what he saw as the power-crazed behaviour of the Italian right-wing leader Mussolini, who shocked the world with racist language in a speech to his army as they prepared for the invasion of Abyssinia: 'Men, remember that black troops have always been defeated by Italians,' he said. Alan was horrified by what he heard and wrote an impassioned newspaper column on the subject: 'To say that, "as the climax of a heroic speech", is to make an exposure of the person at the same time funny, pathetic and shameful; in which attributes it is completely in keeping with the war that inspired it.' He used the same column to define and clarify his political position, which was still the subject of much debate:

I happened to say casually the other day that I was a Liberal,
he went on. *Naturally I was challenged to explain what I meant
by "a Liberal". The only definition I could give was "One who
hates Fascism and Communism equally". The important word
is "equally". I know Conservatives who hate both, and
Socialists who hate both, but I also know under which, if they
had to choose, they would choose to live. To the good Liberal
(if that is what I am) there is no choice possible, for they are the
same thing: the negation of everything which makes life worth
living.*

As 1935 marched on, and war looked increasingly likely, Alan's
worries deepened. In August, Mussolini declared that the Abyssinian
dispute could only be resolved by force, and on 6 September *The Times*
published a despairing letter revealing that Alan was losing his faith
in the League of Nations. He had pinned all hopes of averting war on
the organisation:

*The League of Nations represents man's first fumbling
approach to national decency, designed to include extra-
European nations, solely in order to include America, which
refused to join it. Its covenant demands from its members a
pledge to abstain from war, to which is added a pledge to make
war on any nation which breaks its pledge; to which is added
an assurance that, if one nation breaks this second pledge, the
other nations are allowed to break it too: that is to say, the
covenant assumes dishonourable conduct to be possible and
bases its remedy on the assumption that further dishonourable
conduct is impossible. In short, the League of Nations is a
paradoxical, misshapen absurdity, such as might be expected
from a businessman who had always despised the arts and was
now busy designing the Taj Mahal.*

*The League enshrines a noble idea but a league which
openly rests its policy on force is a league which discounts
honour in advance. Let the present League go, and let the*

nations begin again. Since all pacts and conventions to which Italy has put her name are now proved worthless, let them be cancelled by mutual consents, and let it be recognised in future that a word of honour is worth exactly nothing if you do not trust to it. Let the new League start its career by making a new Treaty of Geneva, whose astonishing feature will be that nations have sacrificed so much in the cause of war shall prove willing to sacrifice something in the cause of peace.

For the truth is that the League of Nations and the millions who support the League of Nations are facing separate problems. The inarticulate, peace loving millions (to whom, after all, belongs the world) are passionately seeking a new way to peace: The League of Nations is asking itself how, on the old system of large armed forces and an exclusively national outlook, it can avoid war.

But even in the middle of what he saw as an extremely serious political discussion, which had absolutely nothing to do with *Winnie-the-Pooh*, he could not escape the children's books. Professor Murray fired off a withering response, damning Alan's suggestion of scrapping the League of Nations, as 'very, very young'.

CHAPTER TWELVE

'A little Consideration, a little thought for others, makes all the difference.'

The outspoken political views, which Alan imagined would distance him permanently from *Winnie-the-Pooh*, only made him even more famous and actually served as excellent publicity. Sales continued to flourish. It had become a phenomenon way beyond his control by this point, and there was nothing to be done about it. At the end of 1935 his American publisher, Dutton's, brought out cheap one dollar editions, creating a new mass market and spreading Alan's popularity yet further still. He vowed to never write for children again, and refused countless requests, until one finally intrigued him. He was persuaded to introduce the English translation of Jean de Brunhoff's children's classic *The Story of Babar*. He had come across the original French edition at a friend's house two years earlier, and had been urging his British publisher to translate the gently satirical stories ever since. He stated that anyone who did not share his love for the elephant tales, which were a novel mix of reality and fantasy, deserved 'to wear gloves and be kept off wet grass for the rest of your life'.

Alan was still firing off letters to *The Times*, identifying himself to readers as 'an ordinary idealistic Englishman', but was becoming disillusioned and felt increasingly powerless. He felt his voice was not being heard, and as German troops entered the demilitarised zone of the Rhineland in 1936, he was plunged into despair. He wrote briefly to his old chum Turley about the worsening international situation, but then turned to the much more pleasant subject of his son instead. To his delight, Christopher was excelling academically and sportingly at Stowe:

The world is foul, he wrote. *I detest Mussolini, I abominate Communism, I – but why go on? At times I wish I were a Norwegian.*

Moon, the Stoic, is in grand form. He got his certificate (if that conveys anything to you) last summer at the age of 14. He also got his Junior Colts. He is now in the Upper School, specialising in Maths. He only just missed playing for his house at fives; he should get his Colts colours next term, and play for the school the year after. If only he would grow a bit. He was in terrific form at the nets in the Christmas holidays, and Sandham and Strudwick both think he's IT. He does The Times crossword every day at school (though not always successfully); and (this is a non-sequitur) is the most completely modest, unspoilt, enthusiastic happy darling in the world. In short, I adore him. At this very moment he is in for a House Golf Competition!

Milne went on to tell Turley how he had spent the past year – 'six months reading and thinking, six months writing' – working on a dramatisation of his favourite novel, Jane Austen's *Pride and Prejudice*. He called his adaptation *Miss Elizabeth Bennet*, since it revolved around the story's heroine of the same name, although he had originally intended to write about the author. His explanation of how the idea had come to him gave a fascinating insight into Alan's writing process, in his mind it was almost as if the characters themselves decided the plotline on his behalf:

The characters began to assemble on the stage, he wrote. Mr and Mrs Austen, Cassandra, the cheery brothers, Uncle Leigh; and at her table in a modest corner, busy, over the chatter, at what the family would call "Jane's writing", Miss Austen herself. Soon she will have to say something. What sort of a young woman is she? What will she say? And as soon as she had said it, I knew that it was just Miss Elizabeth Bennet speaking.

So the play, then, must be about Elizabeth Bennet. It must in fact be a dramatisation of Pride and Prejudice. Was this possible? I read the book again. I read all the other books again. I went back to Pride and Prejudice. Quite impossible, I decided at last, but considerable fun to try. I tried...six months later it was finished; and on the day upon which it was finished I read that a dramatised version of Pride and Prejudice was about to be produced on the New York stage. There was still England. Should one hurry to get the play on with any cast that was available or should one wait for the ideal Elizabeth, now unavailable? In the end the risk was taken; the arrangements were made for the early autumn; the Elizabeth I had always wanted began to let her hair grow; the management; the theatre; the producer, all were there...and at that moment the American version arrived in London.

The American version that scuppered his plans was an adaptation by the writer Helen Jerome, and although the reviews were not particularly favourable, she had beaten Alan to it and her play ran in the West End for some time, meaning his had no chance of being produced in London.

At least *The New Statesman* bothered to review his script: 'This dramatisation is vastly more scholarly than the version now visible at the St James's Theatre. Even Mr Milne trips up occasionally. But these are tiny blemishes compared with the enormities of the American version.'

Miss Elizabeth Bennet enjoyed a fairly successful run at the Liverpool Playhouse, and Alan travelled to the North West to make a brief and modest speech at the opening night, 'in the absence of Miss Austen'. It would be a further eighteen months before he could convince producers to put on the play in London, for a short run at the People's Palace. As a review in the *Observer* pointed out: 'Mr Milne, for the first time in his life, I suppose, has been unlucky.'

Alan had certainly suffered setbacks, heartbreak, and loss, and there had been rare misfortunes in his glittering career, but he was always careful not to show that he minded, and still gave the impression that he was a natural winner. But behind the scenes his Midas touch was starting to tarnish, he no longer found it quite so easy to churn out the hits. He was down, but certainly not out, and he was not ready to give up writing just yet. Alan remained grimly determined to repeat the theatrical successes he had enjoyed years earlier with *Mr Pim Passes By, The Truth About Blayds* and *The Dover Road*. And there would be two more plays, both performed in London and New York, but neither matched up. First was *Sarah Simple*, in which he abandoned any pretence of being serious. He decided, given the bleak state of the world at the time, that audiences wanted nothing but a diversion. The play had a short run at The Garrick Theatre in London and at the Provincetown Playhouse in America, but he was savaged by the critics. One wrote that he 'now writes with about as much maturity as Christopher Robin.' 'The play gives to sex the carnal quality of a game of drop the handkerchief,' mocked another.

In England at the time people were reeling from the shocking abdication of Edward VIII, as a result of his controversial love affair with American divorcee Wallis Simpson. Across the country people were utterly appalled by the lewd nature of the revelations about the king, and following the coronation of his brother George VI, there was little appetite for a play about sexual excesses. Matters were not helped by the fact that Alan's mistress Leonora Corbett was *Sarah Simple*'s leading lady.

At the end of the first performance, Alan took to the stage to address the audience himself: 'We wanted to make you laugh,' he told them. 'You have laughed. There is nothing more to say except Thank You.' He had judged the public mood accurately, they wanted to be amused, but even he was not able to buck the national trend. A review by Charles Morgan in the *New York Times* said that Alan had played a smart move:

It is a speech which might well serve as an epitaph on the English theatre as an imaginative and intellectual force. But Mr Milne knows on which side his bread is buttered. Almost every theatre has been hard hit by the approach of the coronation; a heavy mortality may be expected before the traffic begins to move again and the mob ceases to wander about the streets, gaping at itself; but it is reported that French Without Tears and George and Margaret are running to full houses. Why? Because it is not their purpose to make you feel, see, wonder, imagine or understand. Because they are in no sense a criticism of life. Because they require no effort of their audience, neither thought nor any response to communicated suffering or joy, because they have neither unity or tension, but obtain their effect by a rapid fire of trivial (and clever) wisecracks.

Their purpose is 'to make you laugh' and that is what the English theatre has come to. Look down the current list of plays. There is no tragedy among them; there is no serious romance; there is not one piece whose object is to move its audience. But Mr Milne's play will succeed because its purpose is to have a giggle in every line and, in its own meaningless kind, it is, from the polite English point of view, highly competent.

The confusing play told the story of a man whose young wife had left him several years earlier, but their divorce proceedings were somehow muddled and the couple remained married to each other. When the girl returned, she found her former husband having a fling with a clergyman's widow and pretended she was now prepared to be divorced. But she needed a co-respondent to claim she was being unfaithful with, and in the absence of anyone else, the husband put on a large false moustache and pretended to be a strange man who she met at night at the local inn. In the end, the couple happily reconciled, following a farcical scene which *The New York Times* described as:

In the tradition of soup and false moustaches, extremely successful, and is written not badly but with a special neatness of humour that gives it an impress of style. The rest of the play has the kind of polite, meaningless banter which Mr Milne writes better than most men. In brief he has, as he said in his speech, done what he set out to do. Moreover, plays of this kind have a legitimate place in the theatre. The peril – and the boredom – lies in the everlasting repetition of them. If only we might be allowed to think or feel!

The Times review was in a similar vein, concluding with: 'When there is nothing whatever to say, no one knows better than Mr Milne how to say it.' And *Drama* magazine agreed that it was an excellent example of Alan's: 'Art of making something out of nothing.'

It did not damage his reputation, and eighteen months later, he was still popular enough for his next play, *Gentleman Unknown,* to receive sufficient backing for a production at the St James's Theatre. It was to be his last full-length production. On opening night, Daphne was yet again in New York, but Christopher was there to support his father, joined in a private box by Ken's daughter Angela and their long-standing family friend Anne Darlington. Angela recalled: 'Alas, though it was politely received, it was not a success. The man in the opposite box (a beetle-browed play write-cum-physician) got up and left in the interval. I sat and suffered, really suffered, in silence. I can only imagine how A.A.M. felt.'

How he felt was completely dejected at having another disaster on his hands, and vowed to never subject himself to such a depressing experience again. His mind was still focused more on the issues affecting the real world than the make-believe of the theatre, but as civil war broke out in Spain, and a global conflict looked increasingly likely, it finally dawned on him how powerless his writing really was to change anything significant.

He tried to cheer himself up by taking time away from the pressures of London life. He and Christopher joined Ken's widow Maud and her three younger children Angela, Tim, and Tony, on the first of what would become a series of holidays on the Dorset coast. Daphne went with them once, but clearly it was not her scene and she much preferred the Mediterranean sunshine of Capri or Toarmina in Sicily.

Christopher enjoyed those holidays with his cousins, but was concerned that his father was having some kind of mid-life crisis at the time, and using him as a replacement for his late brother, whom he still missed so deeply:

He, I now suspect, saw me as a sort of twin brother, perhaps a sort of reincarnation of Ken, Christopher revealed later. *He needed me to escape from being fifty. It was a private dream of his, but he did once share it. I say once but I really mean in one place. The place was Dorset. Quite naturally, quite unself-consciously, we skipped, back through the years to our schooldays. I would put our age at about twelve. Five twelve year-olds playing happily together. I don't for a moment think that this was done deliberately in order to level out our assorted ages. Nor do I think it was my father who led us back. I think it just happened because we were all Milnes and this is a thing Milnes can do. We do it without effort and we do it for our own private delight.*

For us, to whom childhood has meant so much, the journey back is short, the coming and going easy.

Maud however, was only a Milne by marriage, so was not included in the 'five twelve year-olds'. Christopher explained the family dynamic: 'Maud presided. She was mother of us all, a regal figure moving quietly in the background. Maud, aged about fifty, remained fifty. The rest of us became children.'

Maud's eldest daughter Marjorie was married with a small child of her own and did not go on those holidays. They were joined at various times by other friends including Anne Darlington and Angela's boyfriend, the New Zealand Olympic runner Jack Lovelock. They rented the coastguard's cottage at Osmington, Alan paid for everything of course, and he and Christopher would be driven down together by their long-serving chauffeur Burnside. Angela remembered her beloved uncle arriving 'in a pale blue bow tie, making his eyes very blue, and I think a grey suit. It could hardly have been pale blue, yet that is how I think of it.' She also fondly recalled sunbathing with Alan on the flat roof of the cottage, and running a striped beach towel up the flagpole every morning. Together they would make their way across the cliff tops to the beach where they would tackle *The Times* crossword together, picnicking on ginger nuts: Recalling the rare occasions Alan was able to completely relax she added:

> *We spent much time Looking for Pebbles, not that there weren't plenty but we looked for special kinds, having competitions and shows with different classes eg: leg of mutton or joint of beef class, there being stones that look like cuts of meat. We threw pebbles at A.A.M.'s hat on a stick.*

Back at the cottage Alan would entertain his son, niece, and nephews with imaginative games that required them all to gather up on the roof and try to guess who would be the next person to appear over the hill. He invented the dreaded character of Mitler, an evil villain based on Hitler and the landlord of the local pub, the Picnic Inn. The family was all together at Osmington when the news filtered through that Hindenburg had died and Hitler announced that he would from that moment on be known as Fuhrer and Reich Chancellor and Supreme Commander of the Armed Forces, demanding the entire nation take an oath of unconditional obedience not just to Germany, but also to him personally. Alan was deeply uneasy but managed to joke: 'It was a proud day for Mitler.'

Alan also kept them entertained in the evenings with amusing drawings of princes, swords and dragons: 'He drew quite well in a maddish way and we probably played the picture game the most,' said Angela. But as soon as he returned to London, and Christopher had gone back to his boarding house at Stowe, Alan was engulfed by gloom once again. There seemed little reason for optimism, and he found himself looking back far more often than he could look forward. He came to the conclusion that the time might be right to finally bow to the pressure he was under from his publishers, as well as his army of fans around the world, to start work on his autobiography. Alan received stacks of letters bombarding him with questions about *Winnie-the-Pooh*, but they were usually pushed aside, unanswered:

CHAPTER TWELVE

I can well remember seeing them on the breakfast table every morning and watching him open them, Christopher recalled. *There were letters from students requesting biographical details; there were letters from children wanting autographs; letters from hopeful imitators asking for advice on how to get their books published; letters from Secretaries of Societies requesting his presence at some function or other; even occasional letters from people down on their luck, short of cash and grateful for anything that could be spared. He would read them silently, and pass them, one at a time, to my mother.*

It was not that he was being unkind by not replying, but it took a long time for him to believe that people were really that interested in him, and in a typically modest letter to his former school master H.G. Wells, he wrote: 'I am writing my autobiography and enjoying it as certainly nobody else will: which I take to be the main object of writing.'

Alan had long ago given up writing for profit, he had more money than he could ever spend in his lifetime thanks to the success of *Winnie-the-Pooh*, so he wrote his memoirs at a leisurely pace for his own pleasure. He no longer needed to be concerned about book sales or holding the attention of a theatre audience, nor did he have the pressures of casting or any of the financial or production headaches that went with opening a play. He could enjoy the process, without anyone to worry about but himself.

When it was eventually finished, Alan called his autobiography *It's Too Late Now* and wrote in the introduction:

In this book, as in everything which I have written, I have humoured the author. Whatever happens to the public; the author is not going to be bored. I have enjoyed looking back on the past, and if others now find enjoyment in looking over my shoulder, I am as glad as my publishers will be.

His American publishers objected to the title, and renamed it *What Luck!* for serialisation in *Atlantic Monthly* magazine. Dutton's wanted to publish it simply as *Autobiography* but Alan disagreed, feeling it was open to misinterpretation. He lobbied for the US market to stick with his original, and preferred title, which he argued perfectly expressed the theory that he had subscribed to all his life:

> *Heredity and environment make the child, he insisted. And the child makes the man, and the man makes the writer; so that it is too late now.*
>
> *It does not mean that if I had my life again I should be an engineer or a clergyman or a stockbroker or a better man, and that unfortunately it is too late now to be any of those things.*

But it was far too late for him to be anything but the slightly prudish man he had always been:

> *When I am told, as I so often am, that it is time I 'came to grips with real life' – preferably in a brothel or a public bar, where life is notoriously more real than elsewhere, minds more complex, more imaginative, more articulate, souls nearer the stars – I realised sadly that, even if I made the excursion, I should bring back nothing but the same self to which objection has already been taken.*

Alan never particularly enjoyed the dirty jokes told by his pals at school and university, and preferred golf and gardening to 'drink and fornication'. Indeed, when he took the young actress Fabia Drake for dinner at the Savoy she was delighted to find he that he did not have the same intentions as most other men: 'I was prudish myself,' she said.

Alan's own account of his life was clean and bright, cheerfully avoiding the darker episodes he had endured including Ken's early death, Barry's deviousness over his father's will, and Daphne's romantic entanglements. He focused instead on his wonderful childhood, and the incidents and characters that inspired him. He decided that people would want to know: 'What accident, what environment, what determination placed them where they are?' He wrote at length about his early years, his schooldays and time as a student in Cambridge; but deliberately devoted only a handful of pages to the four famous children's books – even though he was sharply aware that was the section that interested people the most.

Neither his American nor English publishers expected sales to be particularly high, since people had their minds on far more serious matters. Given the political climate, poor figures were predicted and Methuen asked Milne, through his agent Curtis Brown, if he would accept an advance of just £375, rather than the £1,000 that was initially agreed. Alan did not argue, and accepting the lower fee was seen by Methuen as 'A most generous gesture at such a difficult time as this.'

Sales were disappointing that first Christmas as people feared uncertain months ahead, but over time the book sold surprisingly well. The reviews were glowing and C.W. Chamberlain at Methuen wrote to his staff at the publishing house saying: 'Yes, I do agree that the notices for *It's Too Late Now* have been wonderfully good, and there is an excellent one by Robert Lynd in today's *News Chronicle*. I feel pretty certain that we shall soon have to reprint.'

Among the reviews, *The Times Literary Supplement* said: 'The autobiography of this independent and unrepentant writer is further testimony to his originality.' *The New York Herald Tribune* said it was 'the happy life of a happy author,' and found 'much of it downright witty, deeply felt, admirably written, and studded with excellent portraits.' The critic Lewis Gannett admitted that he was among those who had recited Alan's poems to his children so many times 'after which I could recite them with my eyes shut'. But, like many reviewers, he could not fail to notice that Alan actually revealed very little of his 'essential self', and avoided the juicy subjects that he knew people wanted to know about: 'Like his own *Mr Pim*, he passes by at the very moment one would like to have him sit down and talk,' reported the *New York Post*.

Charles Graves, Alan's former colleague from *Punch*, called it 'a mean, ungenerous and untruthful record,' taking particular exception to the unflattering remarks about the magazine's old editor Owen

Seaman. And in *The New Statesman*, Cyril Connolly found himself getting quite angry at the lack of controversy or emotion in Alan's life story, which he said lacked intimacy and complained about its

> *...gentlemanly good taste which veils both a shrewd eye on the main chance and perhaps a fear of life. He reminds me of Noel Coward, a pre-war Noel Coward springing from the same unexpectedly lower middle class stock, but moving with pre-war acceleration into a smooth heaven of light verse, cricketing weekends, good society, whimsical taste and money, money, money. How fond A.A. Milne is of it! Cheques and success in all around he sees.*

Connolly could not understand why, 'there is never an unkind word for anyone', and wondered 'what Christopher Robin himself is like now, and what he would make of it.'

Christopher was relieved at making only the briefest appearance in his father's autobiography, and grateful that nothing more was being added to the legend of his childhood. But he suffered a few unwanted remarks as a result of Alan's revelation that his son was almost named Rosemary. Everything else was conventional and unsurprising, Alan portrayed himself as the pipe-smoking, golf-playing Englishman that everyone always imagined him to be.

When the book was published in September 1939, three weeks after war was declared, Christopher was no longer a child, he was 19 years old and, having left Stowe, joined his father for a holiday at the Bullaven Farm Hotel near Ivybridge on the edge of Dartmoor. Christopher exceeded all his father's expectations by winning an impressive scholarship to Trinity, his former college at Cambridge, and was even to have Alan's old rooms at Whewell Court. Although he had been badly bullied at school, there appeared to be no teenage rebellion, and they were still very close, as Christopher put it: 'Adoring him, admiring him, accepting his ideas.' Christopher was painfully shy, trembled and stuttered, which he later suggested may have been the outward signs of a fear that he could never fulfil his father's deep-seated ambitions for him, and that he would never again be the charming, adorable and competent child that the world imagined Christopher Robin to be. For most people, the boy never really grew up at all:

At the age of eight – and not altogether surprisingly – my voice had begun to get itself knotted up, Christopher said. By the age of twelve, though I was fluent on occasions, there were other occasions when the words got themselves sadly jammed. By the age of sixteen the jamming had got worse and my shyness wasn't helping things. Grandfather Milne could at least say "Good morning"; I would have stuck at the "G", and aware of an insurmountable "G" approaching me down the road, I would have hurried up a side street to avoid it. What does a parent do in such circumstances? Does he (for example) say "If you want it you must go and buy it yourself?" Or does he say "All right, let's go and buy it together?" Rightly or wrongly it was the latter that my father did, and I blessed him for it and loved him all the more.

Before the rift deepened between them, Alan and Christopher clung to their close relationship and exchanged frequent letters, not just during his years at Cambridge but throughout the war too. They were sitting together at Cotchford Farm on 3 September 1939 when they heard Prime Minister Neville Chamberlain's sombre voice on the BBC, declaring that Britain was now at war with Germany. They were words the entire nation had dreaded.

Alan abandoned his political rantings, and wrote in quiet despair: 'It seems impossible to me now that any sensitive man could live through another war. If not required to die in other ways, he would waste away of soul sickness.' Although he had no choice but to face up to the inevitability of war, Alan did not need to be involved physically this time and retreated to the refuge of his study and garden, after writing to the Ministry of Information offering his services: 'It is not easy for a writer to convince himself that the little he can do is all he can do. He has not devoted himself to his profession for so many years, nor esteemed it so highly, that he can now lay it on one side.'

Alan could not understand why people were treating Hitler, Goering and Mussolini as politicians, rather than 'blood-stained criminals', but at that stage he still would not let himself believe that the war would last long enough for Christopher to be called up. He was wrong. Christopher was drafted into the forces right before he could complete his course at Cambridge. Alan wrote to him constantly, first when he was based at an army training camp at Newark, before moving on to Barton Stacey in Hampshire, Aldershot, and then Sible Hedingham in Essex. As a bright and eager young engineer he was later dispatched to the Middle East, North Africa and Italy. In the army, Christopher was given the chance he longed for to distance himself from his famous father. He finally put his difficult childhood behind him, and said that those five years 'provided me with a foundation stone, strong and lasting, on which to build my adult life.'

Though Sussex was far from the frontlines, there was no way Alan could sit quietly at home, throughout the turbulence of the war he dispatched regular letters from Cotchford to *The Times*. When the fighting broke out in 1939 he was at pains to point out that not all Germans were supporters of Hitler's far right wing politics:

May I, then, urge the necessity of making it clear at once, not only that we differentiate now between the Nazi government and the German people, but that through all the horrors and the heat of war we shall continue to differentiate. An honourable peace will be negotiated gladly at any moment with an elected assembly representative of the German people. As the first point in our peace terms let us proclaim unequivocally that a totalitarian state can have no place in a civilised world. Our leaders have been accustomed to say that a nation's form of government is its own concern. It is not; it is the very great concern of its neighbours.

We are fighting not to make the world safe for democracy but because we are convinced that only by democracy can the world be saved, only under democracy can the world live at peace.

To Alan's mind it was not just Britain's democracy at stake, but the future peace of the whole world and restoring civilisation and humanity to Europe. He was alarmed when the US Ambassador to London Joseph Kennedy made a startling statement on his resignation, vowing to keep America out of the war. Alan feared the Americans saw the war as just a European dispute, regardless of the devastating effect that might have on other nations who needed their help. Kennedy's speech included the words: 'My plan is to devote my efforts to what seems to me the greatest cause in the world today and means, if successful, the preservation of the American form of democracy. That cause is to help the President keep the United States out of the war.'

Alan pleaded with the Americans to help. He wrote again to *The Times*, two years after the outbreak of war, urging America to join the Allied Forces bid to defeat the Nazis:

It seems strange to me that in two years of exhortation the moral argument has never been emphasised as the principal argument – and to a pacifist the only argument – for American entry into the war. Continuously America has been urged to take part in a war of self-interest: never has she been summoned to take part in a crusade. Just for a moment, then, on this second anniversary of a fight for Humanity Against Bestiality, I ask Americans to try to visualise what has been happening to Poland for the last two years; to let their minds dwell, if only for a moment, on such a fantasy of horror, such a nightmare of cruelty, as the world has never known. What are they going to do about it? Are they content that this horror should spread over the world – so long as it stops short of America?

Since when have American lives had this special value to Heaven? Would an American mother have her son watch a baby drown while he wonders what its nationality is? What a travesty of American manhood! How has a great and proud country been allowed to proclaim herself so falsely?

He begged America to lend its mighty power, not just on behalf of Britain, but also 'on behalf of those countries whose sufferings have been so much greater'. He tried his best to convince them that 'vital national interests are involved'.

Although he still described himself as a pacifist, Alan felt sure America's involvement could bring the war to an end, and in May 1941 he wrote a lengthy statement in a political pamphlet entitled *War Aims Unlimited*: 'For a pacifist the only legitimate war aim is complete military victory and the only legitimate peace aim the abolition of war.' Alan argued that it was useless trying bring any fascist leader to the negotiating table, and backed up that theory by quoting Mussolini who famously said: 'Fascism does not believe in the possibility or utility of perpetual peace.'

Alan often found himself forced to defend his position, both in private and public. While he very rarely answered any of the letters he received about *Pooh*, he felt differently about his mailbag now and spent many hours composing lengthy responses. Describing the four kinds of letters the postman usually delivered, he said:

1. Surely you believe that we are right to take part in this war?
2. It is not the duty of Pacifists to concern themselves, not with this war but only with the peace that shall follow it?
3. You do still believe, don't you, that all war is wicked and that we are right to resist this one, and insist on an immediate peace.
4. I hear that you support this war. You are a traitor.

Alan knew that *Peace With Honour* had successfully turned some people into pacifists, but now he agreed that force was the only way to defeat Hitler. It was a tricky position to find himself in, and when faced with the fourth type of letter he had no choice but to alter his original arguments slightly:

CHAPTER TWELVE

I am afraid I am not with you; for I believe that war is a lesser evil that Hitlerism, he wrote in his column Time and Tide. I believe that Hitlerism must be killed before War can be killed. I think that it is more important to abolish War than to avoid or stop one war. I am a practical pacifist. In 1933 when I began Peace With Honour my only (infinitesimal) hope of ending war was to publish my views and hope that they would have time to spread before war broke out. They did not. One must try again. But since Hitler's victory will not abolish war; and since Peace now (which is the recognition of Hitlerism) will not abolish war; one must hope to be alive to try again after England's victory – and in the meantime to do all that one can to bring that about.

Many accused him of hypocrisy, but as Alan saw it he had no choice but to campaign for the conflict for end, and he had taken a similar view when the First World War began back in 1914. He added in *Time and Tide*:

To say, when one's country is at war, "I refuse to take any part in war" is as meaningless as to say, when one's house is on fire, "I refuse to take any part in this fire." The fire is there, the war is there, and since one is there oneself, one is part of it. The only escape is suicide. If one remains alive, one must adapt oneself to the circumstances in some other way than by proclaiming that one doesn't approve of arson.

His outspoken views resonated with many people, and were gathering support. The Ministry of Information took him up on his offer to help the war effort by writing for the troops. He produced a pamphlet to be read by British soldiers going into Europe, and was amazed to paid twenty-five guineas for five weeks' work: 'I didn't expect to be paid at all,' he admitted. 'I was proud indeed that at my age my services could be of use in wartime.' The pamphlet was designed to clearly set out the reasons for fighting in the war, to reassure any men who might be having doubts. He listed them as:

1. To deliver the victims of oppression.
2. To save our own country from the fate of the oppressed.
3. To ensure that no country shall ever again have reason to fear the oppressor.
These are the things for which we are fighting. If they are not worth fighting for, then nothing is worth fighting for, he added.

His aim was to explain to the troops exactly what the politicians ordering them into battle meant by oppression:

Those who escape the slave-market and the brothel, the firing squad and the concentration camp, are slowly starving. In all records of barbaric invasion, in all the tales of man's inhumanity to man, in all the blood stained, tear-blotted pages of fiction or history, there has been nothing to equal the profound suffering which Hitler has brought upon occupied Europe.

He went on to motivate soldiers further by outlining his hopes for the heroes who would be returning to a very different Britain after they had helped end the war. In his explanation, Alan likened England to

a beautiful house crammed to the ceilings with furniture and books, some valuable, some rubbish, all of it in hopeless confusion, crowded in anywhere without taste or method. You feel vaguely that you might do something about it someday, but it will be tiring job (and you have, or think you have, a weak heart). You wake up one night to find the house on fire. Frantically you throw out of the windows or drag out of the doors as much of its contents as you can. You save most of them, and in saving them make two discoveries: Your possessions have been brought into the light, and you know now exactly what things of value you have and what of rubbish; moreover you realise that exertion is not so fatal as you had supposed. If the fire brigade can conquer the flames, your house, when restored, will be as beautiful as ever outside; but now, for the first time you will exert yourself to see that the inside is in keeping with it.

But Alan was only too aware that the declaration of peace, when it eventually came, would not bring an end to the suffering. He pointed out that post-war Britain would be dealing with the aftermath of the conflict for a long time to come, including feeding, clothing and housing displaced Europeans, as well as what he described as: 'the recovery of the deported, the search for the missing, the identification of the murdered.'

All he could do was hope that in the future British people would show their compassionate side. Again accurately reflecting the mixed feelings that were sweeping a turbulent nation at the time, Alan hoped for: 'A Britain not entirely devoted to her own interests; a chivalrous Britain; a Britain who has made mistakes in the past but who has redeemed them and will continue to redeem them.'

CHAPTER THIRTEEN

'It is hard to be brave, when you are only a Very Small Animal.'

Aside from a few political articles, letters to newspapers and pamphlets for the Ministry of Information, Alan had little appetite for work as the war raged on. He told his editors at Methuen that he was working on a new novel but it would be 1946 before it was published, and in the meantime Alan amused himself by practicing his long-neglected talent for amusing verse, in a series of poems for *Punch*. *High Purpose* and *The Third String* were the first he had submitted to his former employers in years, and were the start of a series of thirty-six poems that were published in a book together towards the end of 1940 as a kind of informal war diary entitled *Behind The Lines*.

Throughout the war, Alan continued to argue strongly against the idea of any totalitarian state – communist as well as fascist – and tore into Stalin, especially after what he saw as Russia's pointless attack on Finland:

> *Why was it utterly right for Russia to drop bombs on a friendly country to obtain the bases she wanted? he asked. Because everybody knows that everything is all quite different if Russia is doing it. The Communists would accept that the moon was made of green cheese if Stalin said it was or that it would be if it were to the advantage of Communism that it should be, or if the inferior quality of the cheese could be attributed to Capitalism.*

His scornful description of a typical Communist may have had something to do with the disastrous state of his marriage at the time:

CHAPTER THIRTEEN

He has a woman's capacity of ignoring all inconvenient facts,
of assuming a special dispensation from the laws of logic, of
demanding as by right the best of both worlds, and of doing all
this with a naive unawareness that anyone is noticing it, or if
noticing it, can be so unreasonable as to object.

Keen to publicise his loathing of communism, Alan came up with the
additional idea of adding some comments to each new poem to explain
their meaning in greater depth when *Behind The Lines* was published.
He explained to C.W. Chamberlain:

By the time they come out, they will be neither urgently topical,
nor "untopical". But what they will be is a record of the first
eight months of the war, and, so to speak, historical. It has
suddenly come into my mind that it would be "fun", useful,
interesting, attractive, to add a prose postscript to each poem.
In some cases it might be no more than an explanation of some
reference whose point would now be forgotten, or a reminder
of the occasion which prompted the verses; in others I might
elaborate the theme, defend my attitude, or embroider with
anecdote ("in Mr Milne's inimitable style", thank you). This
would bring the book more into the "war-diary" class; which
is the one sort of book which can never be out of date: the more
"out of date", in fact, the more interesting. See what I mean?
Tell me if you like the idea. I think it gives the book an
attraction which verses (alone) lack for many people.

Needless to say, Methuen leapt at the chance to publish more of
Milne's poetry, as there had been a desperate demand for it ever since
Winnie-the-Pooh. His publishers felt sure they were sitting on a
goldmine, and when Alan sent the manuscript off to his typist on 4
July 1940, Chamberlain waited with bated breath. But the tone was
misjudged and he chose to make light of remarkably inappropriate
subjects, including the Russian invasion of Finland, the Nazi-Soviet
pact and blackouts during the Blitz, and of course he targeted Stalin:

'So all is well, and Stalin's right
And will be right until he's dead,
And black is obviously white
If each alternately is red:
A helpful creed, whose only hitch
Is knowing when the one is which.

He also tackled the awkward subject of Londoners having to find drawing pins to attach their blackout blinds to the windows each night before the enemy bombing campaign began:

Each night the same old argument begins.
We reach the same old impasse every night:
We can't turn on the light without the pins,
We cannot find the pins without the light.

While many other poets at the time were seeking to glorify war, that was a concept that sickened Alan who wanted to destroy the conventional belief that war was an honourable way of settling international disputes, although he had come to the conclusion that it was impossible to try to negotiate with Hitler: 'If anyone reads *Peace With Honour* now, he must read it with that one word HITLER scrawled across every page,' he wrote. 'One man's fanaticism has cancelled rational argument.'

Alan fervently hoped his readers would come to see modern warfare just as he did, as: 'something as far removed from the Napoleonic Wars as they were from a boxing match'. He was adamant that there was no hope for democracy unless fascism was defeated entirely, and found himself unable to lend his support to the growing numbers of conscientious objectors. He included an angry poem entitled *The Objector*, which included the controversial lines:

Your Conscience thinks the war should cease
But finds no fault with German peace
Accepting with a careless nod

142

CHAPTER THIRTEEN

The kingdom of its anti-God.
It minds not who seduces whom
If, safe within its narrow room,
It still can hug itself and say
"We took no part in war today";
It will not mind who lost, who won,
So long as you have fired no gun.

After it appeared in *Punch* he was inundated with letters from conscientious objectors, but Alan, who abhorred everything about war, argued that they had a duty to protect the hundreds of thousands of children being left frightened, hungry, orphaned, wounded, or dead. In his opinion, objectors were in the same position as a man who says to his family:

Although we are in danger of starvation, my conscience does not allow me to steal. But I do not reproach you for stealing, since your conscience does allow you to. So I hope you will be thoroughly more successful in your efforts tonight, and then we can all have a good meal.

I think that there is a difference between refusing to "use the sword" to defend oneself and refusing to use it to defend the innocent and helpless. I cannot believe that, if Christ in His journeys had come across a sadist torturing a child, He would have been content to preach a parable. The Conscientious Objector does believe this.

Alan was also tiring of his wife's behaviour, and began dropping more and more hints about his unhappy personal life. In a newspaper article deploring the fact that there seemed to be one law for the rich and another for the poor, he openly mocked wealthy women like Daphne and her society friends who frequented high-end London department stores. He wrote how unfair it was that a poor woman who steals bread for her children would end up in prison, while

143

...the rich woman, who tries to collect a vanity case without paying for it, is certified by a Harley Street specialist as suffering from a nervous breakdown (due to the fact that she got up at eleven that morning instead of twelve) and is committed (poor soul) to the care of friends, who drop in at cocktail-time to say what a perfect pet the magistrate was.

Mrs Milne was always immaculately groomed, and wore a great deal of make-up, something which baffled her husband who decided to take the opportunity to express his dislike of cosmetics:

The modern world has accepted the convention that obviously painted lips and obviously gummed on lashes are beautiful, he went on. I found myself saying the other day that the extravagances of this cosmetic age proved finally that women adorned themselves for women only, not for men; in proof of which I assured my company that without exception every man I knew preferred a clean face to a painted one.

Daphne would spend hours at the hairdresser or beautician preparing for her many public appearances, and was well known for her extravagant love of shopping and expensive designer clothes, but Alan failed to understand how women could 'spend so many hours every week in the retention of beauty'.

She loved the limelight, and her fashionable wardrobe was the source of much speculation when she swept into Sussex, although despite being the subject of much local gossip herself, she always seemed cheerful and never discussed anything unpleasant. Alan hoped to avoid the difficult subject of their relationship too. During the war he was entirely preoccupied with politics, and he and Daphne rarely discussed matters of the heart anyway. The situation resolved itself since she was not able to travel to America during the war, and in 1940 they left London, which was being ravaged by bombs, and lent the Chelsea house to friends. Moving permanently to Sussex forced the couple to spend more time together than they had in years.

CHAPTER THIRTEEN

With Christopher gone, they filled their long hours by talking about gardening or their mutual devotion to their pets. Life was not the same without their son, and Alan grew increasingly nostalgic, longing for the days when the two of them would play a round of golf together, and then stop off at the pub afterwards for a glass of refreshing ginger beer, before Daphne would walk along the lane to meet them and they would all drive home together. Village life looked very different as it embraced families of evacuees, or refugees as Alan always insisted on calling them. Despite the changing times, they still employed their housekeeper Mrs Wilson and her daughter Pat, but visitors were scarce and the house felt horribly empty. Alan wrote:

> *Shall we have no one (oh, the peace and quiet!)*
> *No one who grumbles, no one hard to please,*
> *Nobody wasteful, fussy, on a diet*
> *Shall we (in short) get back our refugees?*

Once a week he took the train up to London and spent the day having a massage and lunch with his friends or publishers, usually at the Garrick Club. Daphne would go up too, but on a different day, and spend time with her own friends. London was enduring the worst of the blitz bombing, and at times they would arrive to find parts of the city on fire, or completely destroyed. Methuen's offices on Essex Street, near the Strand, were bombed the same week *Behind The Lines* was published, and Chamberlain wrote to Alan:

> *A huge bomb had fallen at the back of the Temple and we had not a pane of glass throughout the rear of our building. All the furniture in Lucas's old room was lying about battered and broken and the whole place was in a deplorable state. For two whole days we had no water and we are still without gas.*

But Sussex did not feel much safer. After the D-Day landings at Dunkirk in June 1940, there was a constant risk of invasion from France, and Cotchford was right in the path of any invading armies

145

advancing on London. As enemy bombers approached the capital, they flew directly over the Milne's farm, and on several occasions released their bombs dangerously close to the house: 'The Luftwaffe never ceases to watch over us, day and night,' Alan wrote to Ken's son Tony in October that year.

Alan dedicated *Behind The Lines* to his son:

> *To my affinity:*
> *C.R. Milne: Mathematical scholar of Trinity:*
> *And: By the time this appears;*
> *With any luck Private in the Royal Engineers.*

But it had not been easy for Christopher to land the job he wanted, and he had to rely on Alan's high level political connections to become an engineer, otherwise known as a 'sapper'. Since he was a child Christopher had a passion for engineering, and from the age of about 7 Alan would have to call on him to fix anything that broke around the house:

> *How did one become a Sapper? That was the question, Christopher wrote. And you may well think it was not one worth bothering an Under Secretary of State about. Indeed, you might well think that a greater problem might have been how to avoid becoming a Sapper.*
>
> *However, this was what I had set my heart on, and we just didn't know whether we could trust the War Office not to post me instead to an Infantry Battalion. In any case there was little else that a middle-aged author could do to help win the war, so my father probably welcomed this opportunity to exert himself on behalf of his son.*
>
> *I can't remember now what was the outcome of his letter. But I do recollect another string he pulled producing a reply from an Engineer Colonel in which he said how much easier it would all have been if I were skilled in some suitable trade. Was I by any chance an amateur bricklayer? And then it was*

that we suddenly saw that my one great qualification was not mathematics but carpentry. "So if the Engineers need a keen carpenter," wrote my father, "he's your man." "And," he added to me, "while waiting to see where that gets us, you must jolly well make yourself as expert as you possibly can. I wonder if there is a helpful book we could get." And, going once more to the top, he wrote to Christina Foyle, the bookseller, to find out.

The book Alan found at Foyle's famous London bookshop was *Modern Practical Carpentry*, and brushing up on a host of new wood-working skills helped Christopher pass his trade test, but it was a close call as he failed the medical at first. During the routine physical examination, Christopher trembled with nerves, just as he had during dozens of school cricket matches, which led doctors to believe he was suffering from a far more serious condition, and he was declared unfit for service.

Christopher recalled the moment he broke the news to Alan:

What does a father do when he learns that his son is not fit for military service? Does he heave a sigh of relief? Maybe mine did, but it would have been a sigh quickly satisfied by an understanding of how I felt about it, and by the thought that here was yet another opportunity for him to do something to help.

It may have been seen as interfering, but Alan wanted to do what he could to resolve the situation, and so he once again used his considerable influence. This time he went straight to the top, sending a letter to the most important doctor in the country, Lord Horder, and the army agreed to take another look at the candidate. It paid off, and in February 1941 Sapper C.R. Milne joined the second training battalion of the Royal Engineers, although he was not commissioned until July 1942 when he was given a week's leave with his parents before setting sail for the Middle East.

The gruelling journey took almost eight months, travelling via Bombay, Basra, and a long uncomfortable stay in Northern Iraq. In a letter to Chamberlain, thanking him for some books, Alan wrote: 'The Libya one, which I enjoyed enormously, has been sent on to C.R.M. who (alas!) is now at sea on his way to that neighbourhood. He got it just before he sailed.'

But Alan feared that, as a result of his own outspoken anti-war beliefs, the letters between him and Christopher were being intercepted and censored. Writing at Christmas 1942 to his niece Marjorie, who spent much of the war caring for evacuated Westminster schoolboys, Alan explained:

On Monday we had an airgraph from Moon dated Nov 17th, saying that he had still had no letters. On Tuesday Mrs Wilson had an airgraph dated December 2nd, thanking her for the socks she had sent him for his birthday. So thank Heaven something has arrived from England; but why no airgraph thanking me for my 92 letters? Sickening. Perhaps the censor is getting busy with it again, Milne now being a suspected name. His last airgraph said that it rained every day and they were all up to the neck in mud, "but I am well and happy so what more can one want?" Remember this, Mrs M-R, when you are up to the neck in somebody else's mumps.

Alan longed for any scraps of information about his son whom he described as, 'a very good and very regular letter-writer luckily, for we miss him terribly, and live from one letter to the next'. Every letter was precious, although any day might bring the news they dreaded most – that he had been injured or killed, and Alan explored his darkest fears in a play called *Tristram* which opened with a father reading his late son's letters in the summer-house at the end of the garden. The story reflected how Alan might cope if the worst happened to Christopher and, like the boy in the play, left a completely unspoilt and untarnished record of their close relationship through a series of loving letters.

CHAPTER THIRTEEN

By the Spring of 1943 Christopher was in Tunisia, having spent time in Tahag, Kirkuk, Baghdad, Zubair, Bombay, and Cape Town: 'When you next find me I may be in Berlin,' he wrote. 'Or coming across the lawn from the garden house.' But it would be another three years before Christopher returned, a very different young man indeed.

The war tested even the closest relationships to breaking point. Alan fell out with his old friend P.G. Wodehouse when the *Jeeves and Wooster* writer made a series of controversial radio broadcasts from Germany at the height of the conflict. Despite forty-nine weeks in prison, he cheerfully urged listeners to end their intolerance towards the Germans. Alan was incensed by what he saw as the ultimate betrayal, and later Wodehouse admitted that with hindsight the five broadcasts, made specifically with American audiences in mind, may have been a mistake:

> *My reason for broadcasting was a simple one,* he explained. *In the course of my period of internment I received hundreds of letters of sympathy from American readers of my books who are strangers to me, and I was naturally anxious to let them know how I had got on.*
>
> *Of course, I ought to have had the sense to see that it was a loony thing to do to use the German radio for even the most harmless stuff, but I didn't. I suppose prison life saps intellect.*

Alan was not the only one infuriated, Auberon Waugh described the broadcasts as having 'about as much political content of any sort as the average Donald Duck or Tom and Jerry cartoon', and George Orwell said: 'In the desperate circumstances of the time, it was excusable to be angry at what Wodehouse did.'

He found it particularly dangerous for Americans, who were still neutral at that stage in the war, to be 'told by a famous and respected figure that he was living very comfortably in Germany and that the Germans were very nice chaps who looked after him admirably'.

Although the two had always admired each other's work, Alan was shocked that Wodehouse completely omitted to mention the Nazi's crimes or concentration camp atrocities. Alan's nephew Tony explained how much his uncle and Wodehouse, known as Plum, actually had in common:

They were born within three months of one another in respectable middle-class families (though Plum's had some blue blood in it) and went to public schools, where they were both goodish games players – cricket and football.

Both knew at an early age that writing was the only thing they wanted to do. Alan refused to take a job; Plum agreed with great reluctance and left as soon as his writing income exceeded his salary (after two years). Both aimed at the light and 'funny' market, with Alan going for sketches and Plum for stories.

Both joined a club – not the same one. Plum hated it and resigned; Alan, though not a truly clubbable man, left a large sum of money to it. Both loved the theatre and wrote for it enthusiastically, while caring little for the cinema, though both made some money out of it. They wanted the same kind of life-style, that is a place to write undisturbed, but both married women who wanted more of a social life than that.

Both made a lot of money but seemed not to care, except in so far as it was a badge of success. Neither had expensive tastes – the wives made up for that. Both loved to play golf. Alan watched cricket; Plum's interest was mainly in schoolboy games, but he followed Tests in the newspapers.

Neither could take foreigners seriously. They both avoided trying to speak languages. Both were single-child parents, Plum a stepfather only. He adored his step-daughter, and Alan was somewhat over protective towards his only son.

The conclusion is perhaps that they both reflected their period and class.

Despite these many similarities between the two, Wodehouse rarely involved himself in international politics, and Alan could not forgive

Wodehouse's betrayal of his country. The whole affair stirred up passionate feelings, and Auberon Waugh who had been disappointed in Wodehouse, ended up with little sympathy for Alan either. He said: 'Within days all the literary creeps in the country from A.A. Milne upwards, had written to the *Daily Telegraph* to demonstrate their own super-patriotism and jealousy of a man whose shoes they were not fit to clean.'

Wodehouse had taken up residence at the luxurious Adlon Hotel in Berlin, from where he made his weekly broadcasts. Alan was horrified, and maintained his angry position in a letter to the *Daily Telegraph*:

> *The news that P.G. Wodehouse has been released from his concentration camp delighted his friends; the news that he had settled down comfortably at the Adlon made them anxious; the news that he was to give weekly broadcasts (but not about politics, because he had "never taken any interest in politics" left them in no doubt as to what had happened to him. He had "escaped" again.*
>
> *I remember that he told me once he wished he had a son; and he added characteristically (and quite sincerely): "But he would have to be born at the age of fifteen, when he was just getting into his House eleven." You see the advantage of that. Bringing up a son throws considerable responsibility on a man. But by the time the boy is fifteen one has shifted the responsibility on the housemaster, without forfeiting any reflected glory that may be about.*
>
> *This, I felt, had always been Wodehouse's attitude to life. He has encouraged in himself a natural lack of interest in "politics" – "politics" being all the things which the grown-ups talk about at dinner when one is hiding under the table. Things, for instance, like the last war, which found and kept him in America; and post-war taxes which chased him backwards and forwards across the Atlantic until he finally found sanctuary in France. An ill-chosen sanctuary it must have seemed last June, when politics came surging across the Somme.*

Irresponsibility in what the papers call "a licensed humourist" can be carried too far; naiveté can be carried too far. Wodehouse has been given a good deal of licence in the past, but I fancy now his licence will be withdrawn.

Before this happens I beg him to surrender it of his own free will; to realise that though a genius may grant himself an enviable position above the battle where civic and social responsibilities are concerned, there are times when every man has to come down to the arena, pledge himself to the cause in which he believes, and suffer for it.

His letter infuriated and offended many people, not least Wodehouse's beloved step-daughter Leonora Cazalet, who said:

It really is horrid about Plummie, and of course not for me to use obscene language about Mr Milne, but I can't help being pleased when other people do it. I feel a bit like a mother with an idiot child that she anyway loves better than all the rest.

Scottish writer Compton Mackenzie, author of *Monarch of the Glen*, felt that Alan had been particularly foolish to bring up the question of Wodehouse's non-existent son:

There is a curious infelicity in Mr A.A. Milne's sneer at P.G. Wodehouse for shirking the responsibility of fatherhood, Mackenzie wrote to the *Daily Telegraph. Such a rebuke would have come more decorously from a father who has abstained from the profitable exhibitionism in which the creator of Christopher Robin has indulged.*

I gather Mr Wodehouse is in disgrace for telling the American public over the radio about his comfortable existence at the Hotel Adlon. Not being convinced that I am morally entitled to throw stones at a fellow author, and retaining as I do an old-fashioned prejudice against condemning a man unheard, I do not propose to inflict my opinion upon the public, beyond affirming that at the moment I feel more disgusted by Mr Milne's morality than by Mr Wodehouse's responsibility.

It later emerged that Wodehouse had never actually made the remark about wanting a 15-year-old son, Alan had read it in his book *Psmith In The* City, and wrongly credited it to the author. Years later when the journalist Richard Usborne pointed the error out to Wodehouse, he replied:

You have cleared up a mystery that has been puzzling me for years. The thing he quoted me as saying seemed familiar, but I was certain I had never said it to him. Odd chap, Milne. There was a curious jealous streak in him which doesn't come out in his writing. I love his writing but never liked him much.

Wodehouse may well have been on to something, Alan was rather jealous of his success as a humourist, and it annoyed him that his own books were so often subject to parody and attack. His nephew Tony subsequently wrote about the Wodehouse affair:

Our hero doesn't come too well out of this. Just as it is now obvious in retrospect that PGW should never have done the broadcasts, so it is obvious that Alan should never have gone as far as he did, accusing his friend of refusing the responsibilities of fatherhood. Some of his fellow writers – Compton Mackenzie for one – expressed their disgust at this betrayal of a friend at a time when silence was called for if support was impossible.

One can say in explanation that 1941 was a bad time for Alan. He had become obsessed with the war and was in no mood to wait for the evidence before shouting "Traitor!" The charge of political naivety could be made against Wodehouse, but it did not become AAM to make it, the same AAM who in the thirties had taken a pacifist stand which – as he later acknowledged – could only have served Hitler's purposes.

Alan could have saved something from the wreck if he had dissociated himself from the disgraceful attack on Wodehouse. But he did not. I hate to think that he may actually have liked it.

Small wonder that PGW looked for discreditable signs in Alan of professional jealousy to explain his conduct, and that he took some mild revenge on Alan thereafter in his writings. I wonder though whether he was being quite truthful when he said he "never liked him much", while still appreciating his work.

Wodehouse loathed Alan after this episode, that much is evident, but remained extremely interested in following his career, and made a point of always finding out what he was working on. He wrote to their mutual friend Denis Mackail in 1945 saying:

I don't know if it is a proof of my saint-like nature, but I find that my personal animosity against a writer never affects my opinion of what he writes. Nobody could be more anxious than myself, for instance, that Alan Alexander Milne should trip over a loose boot lace and break his bloody neck, yet I re-read his early stuff at regular intervals with all the old enjoyment and still maintain that in The Dover Road he produced about the best comedy in English.

Wodehouse took the mildest form of revenge on his old adversary by describing Madeline Bassett, one of his sillier recurring characters in the *Jeeves* stories, as a typical reader of Alan's children's books:

Though externally, as you say, a pippin, she is the sloppiest, mushiest, sentimentalist young Gawd-help-us who ever thought the stars were God's daisy chain and that every time a fairy hiccoughs a wee baby is born. She is squashy and soupy. Her favourite reading is Christopher Robin and Winnie-the-Pooh. I can perhaps best sum it up by saying that she is the ideal mate for Gussie Fink-Nottle,

CHAPTER THIRTEEN

But he did not leave it at that, in his 1949 novel *The Mating Season*, Wodehouse also had Bertie Wooster make himself look even more ridiculous and bumbling than usual by having to recite Alan's poems at a village concert:

It is unnerving to know that in a couple of days you will be up on a platform in the village hall telling an audience, probably well provided with vegetables, that Christopher Robin goes hoppity-hoppity-hop, Bertie observed his in typical style. *A fellow who comes on a platform and starts reciting about Christopher Robin going hoppity-hoppity-hop (or alternatively saying his prayers) does not do so from sheer wantonness but because he is a helpless victim of circumstances beyond his control. While an audience at a village concert justifiably resents having Christopher Robin poems recited at it, its resentment becomes heightened if the reciter merely stands there opening and shutting his mouth in silence like a goldfish. Except for remembering in a broad, general way that he went hoppity-hoppity-hop.*

While his aim was to mock, Wodehouse was inadvertently acknowledging that Alan's stories had become such an integral part of the English language, culture and tradition that any writer could refer to them, simply taking it for granted that everyone had heard of them. Another example was when they received a mention in Richmal Compton's phenomenally popular *Just William* series of children's books. In *William The Pirate*, his arch-enemy Anthony cannot believe that naughty schoolboy William has never heard of Christopher Robin: '"Good heavens!" Anthony exclaims. "I shouldn't have thought there was anyone...I simply can't make out how you've never come across those books. They're everywhere." It was clear that he felt a true missionary zeal to convert them to his cult.'

Over a period of twenty years, the *Winnie-the-Pooh* stories had become modern folk stories, and a game of Poohsticks, what Tiggers like to eat or an Expotition to the North Pole required no further explanation.

CHAPTER FOURTEEN

'Just because an animal is large, it doesn't mean he doesn't want kindness.'

Alan was firmly established as an international superstar of the literary world, but no matter how hard he tried, or whatever else he wrote, it was Christopher Robin and Pooh who had captivated everybody's hearts. Even his great friend Frank Swinnerton, who had known Alan for many years and should have known how much it might annoy him, compared him to *Peter Pan* author J.M. Barrie. In his book *The Georgian Literary Scene*, Swinnerton said he may have been popular but he certainly was not fashionable:

Milne is so far out of the literary fashion that he failed to detest his parents, he wrote. *His parents had previously failed to ill-treat and misunderstand him. He failed to detest his school and his schoolfellows. He failed to have furtive adolescent misadventures which left him with burning hatred of all females and an illicit love for some fellow male.*

He married early, and his marriage failed to be a failure. He had one son, who failed to disappoint or to hate him. And his life has failed to be disagreeable in every particular perhaps because he has failed to be as unpleasant as possible to every person he met.

In appearance Milne is extraordinarily fair. He is of the middle height – perhaps a little above it – and to this day is as slim as when he first came down from Cambridge. His eyes are very blue, his face is thin but not pale, and I think it would impossible to see him without realising at once that he has an active and quickly – smoothly – working mind. There are authors who look stupid and angry; nobody could miss the

156

intelligence of Milne's expression, and the ready but not especially effulgent kindness of his agreeable smile. An observer who knew nothing of his books and plays would probably discover that the face was notably keen and handsome, free from any sign of malice or cruelty, but lacking in what I may call the lines of boisterousness. He would not at first, I think, find it easy to understand what Milne said, owing to the inaudibility and little slurring quickness of his speech. He would notice that, like Barrie, Milne is devoted to the game of cricket. What else he would notice I do not know.

Unlike the man whose mind is occupied, then, Milne does not tirelessly volunteer conversation. Nor, however, does he repress it in others, as do the haughty; a fact from which I draw an inference concerning Milne the writer as well as Milne the man. The inference is that while plentifully blessed (as Barrie had been) with fancy, and even more plentifully blessed than Barrie with verbal adroitness (as witness his versification), he does not command that gift of the great romancers and novelists, a profuse fecundity of invention. Although by no means unappreciative of these traits in other men, he is deficient in vulgarity, in energy, in largeness of thought, and in exuberance of action.

Needless to say, Alan had no complaints at such a detailed and flattering portrait painted by Swinnerton, and was equally delighted when he heard that Penguin planned to publish a selection of his lightest plays, entitled *Four Plays*, containing *Have The Honour, Belinda, The Dover Road*, and *Mr Pim Passes By* – which remained many people's favourite. And *The Pocket Milne*, a selection of his comic sketches, was published in December 1941. In his introduction, which Alan had written the previous Christmas, he recalled how difficult it had been to shake off his former *Punch* persona:

For years afterwards he was always in the picture; posing at one time as a model to which I was failing to live up, at another as an artist's proof that nothing which I was saying ought to be taken seriously. In fact, he became, as one's past is apt to become, both a rival and a millstone. This little book contains the best of what my rival was writing thirty years ago.

His autobiography was still proving popular too. C.W. Chamberlain told Alan in April 1943 that he expected to sell 2,500 more copies of *Those Were The Days* by the end of the year after bringing out a new, cheaper edition. And a new edition of *The Red House Mystery* sold 3,000 copies the same year. As usual, Methuen could not keep up with the demand for the children's books, struggling to find enough paper to keep them in print when rationing took effect during the war. They repeatedly had to explain to Alan that the shortage meant that all four books were out of stock 'for a good many weeks' but they planned to print 25,000 more copies of each as soon as they possibly could. Chamberlain wrote: 'With your famous 'four' we are rationed to under five hundred of each, and even then the binder sometimes lets us down. Had we been able to get a thousand per week of each, we could easily have sold them.'

For the first time, the sales of *Winnie The Pooh* were almost exactly the same as for *When We Were Very Young*, with *The House At Pooh Corner* not far behind in third place, and *Now We Are Six* the least popular, but it still sold an impressive 8,554 copies in the first six months of 1941. They were not simply maintaining their sales, but increasing in popularity as time went on, which was almost unheard of in publishing.

Chamberlain added: 'I only hope we shall we able to keep sufficient stock to meet the demand over Xmas, but the problem of production gets greater and greater.'

There were similar surges in sales all around the world every Christmas. In Sweden, a country which remained politically neutral throughout the war, sales soared during the conflict, selling an astonishing 5,000 copies every year until 1946. In 1943 the decision was made to print 4,000 copies of each of the four titles in Australia in a bid to meet the growing demand: 'We can get the books produced in Melbourne and offered to the public at precisely the same price as when we ship our own stock there,' Chamberlain told his most profitable author.

Despite being a household name, Alan was often able to fly under the radar, and enjoyed telling a typically self-deprecating story about how he was rarely recognised in public:

One day during the war, having to be in London for various reasons, I went into a large store to buy a sponge. We pumped our own water at that time, so we could not complain of its quality, but it was death to sponges. The price of a sponge has always come as something of a shock to me. One feels that one should get for one's own money something more regular in shape, with fewer holes in it.

I chose a large healthy specimen, once, no doubt, the pride of the reef. Its price was wired on to it; otherwise I should have supposed the figure to be a rough valuation of the department, possibly the whole store. I gave the assistant my name and address.

The girl's face lit up. This does happen sometimes, and on the rare occasions when it does, my face lights up too. It was pleasant to think she had read my books, or (more probably) knew somebody who had. We smiled at each other in a friendly way, and she said that I must be feeling proud of myself. I gave a modest imitation of a man who prefers to have it said rather than to say it.

"Taking a holiday now?" she asked.

This puzzled me a little. One need not take a long holiday in order to buy a sponge; and, of course, if one had known the price, one would have known that one couldn't afford to. However, I gave her another smile, and went to another department to buy a pair of slippers.

It was to a man this time that I gave my name and address. His face also lit up; so, of course, did mine. Never before had I been such a public character. He said "Well, you've been doing a fine bit of work." Had I known him better, I should have asked him to which manifesto or pamphlet he was referring, for one likes to be told these things. As it was, I said with a shrug "Oh well, we must all do what we can." He agreed.

"Got it all in?" he went on. This baffled me. It seemed to be, but could hardly be, a low reference to the nominal fee which I accept sometimes for these things. But before I could answer, he added and put the afternoon at last in its true perspective: "We owe a lot to you farmers."

After all these years of authorship it is disheartening to find that it is not one's name but one's address which raises admiration in the breasts of strangers. Yet if one is to be mistaken for what one is not, I would as soon be thought a farmer as anything.

Indeed I have sometimes played with the idea of making this place a farm again, but the amount of writing which it would involve has stayed me. I do enough writing anyway.

When the army asked to requisition his field at Cotchford Farm, Alan was horrified by volume of paperwork he was expected to complete, including sixty questions about the history of the land, its rotation of crops for the previous six years, and even its outgoings on 'artificial manures'. In the end he simply handed the field over as a gift instead of bothering to fill out the forms.

His story about buying the sponge made up just one of many articles Alan was commissioned to write for the *New York Times* about life in wartime England. Other subjects he tackled in an equally amusing fashion included the evacuees they offered a home to at the farm, the sporadic bombing, the Home Guard, the limitation of dried egg and the prevalence of pilchards as a result of rationing – after that particular article appeared he was sent regular food parcels from concerned American readers.

By February 1943, sick of the on-going war, Alan was deeply disappointed when the historic meeting in Casablanca between Prime

Minister Winston Churchill and US President Franklin D Roosevelt failed to lead to a plan to defeat the enemy nations – Germany, Italy, Japan, Hungary, Romania and Bulgaria – which had become known as the Axis powers. The Allied powers were Britain, the US, France, USSR, Australia, Belgium, Brazil, Canada, China, Denmark, Greece, Netherlands, New Zealand, Norway, Poland, South Africa and Yugoslavia. Alan expressed his fury at the lack of progress towards peace in yet another of his strongly worded letters to *The Times*: 'I could have wished that Casablanca had produced, not only final plans for the defeat of the Axis, but some statement to the enemy of what that defeat would mean.'

Despairing of the politicians, he came up with his own detailed six-point plan which he felt certain would hasten the end of the war:

The peace dictated by the Allies will make any subsequent war of revenge by the Axis utterly and finally impossible, he explained. Apart from this, its main purpose will be to give the German and Italian people an equal opportunity with the rest of the world to enjoy the Four Freedoms: freedom from want, freedom from fear, freedom of religion, freedom of expression. The complete victory of the Allies can be delayed but cannot now be prevented. In light of the allied intentions here set out it is for every German and every Italian to wonder whether any advantage to himself or his country will be gained by delay.

And he went on to suggest:

A potent propaganda which would show both our might and our mercy and will do much to split the people from the party in a Germany and Italy where growing depression must mean growing disillusionment.

Alan's greatest concern, needless to say, was for the safety of his son who was making a long and hazardous journey from Iraq towards Tunisia. He was part of an immense caravan of thousands of soldiers, and hundreds of lorries carrying guns and bridging equipment, heading directly into the line of fire. Christopher did his best to calm his parents' worries by sending cheerful letters home as often as he could. When his battalion stopped in Transjordan that spring he picked them 'a tiny anemone, the brightest crimson, like a drop of blood'. Many weeks later it finally arrived at the farm, drier and paler, but appreciated more than he could possibly have imagined.

Despite the gruelling conditions and physical hardships, Christopher always managed to make his letters sound optimistic and upbeat, and found writing home very comforting: 'In my letters I could write about my home-coming, as certain now that I would one day see Cotchford again as I had before been certain that I would not.' He clung to small but significant details that convinced him peace was not far off. In one letter sent from Benghazi he told his parents: 'Next to the corpse of a German tank, I found a lark's nest bubbling over with young life. War and peace, side by side, the one however devastating never able to obliterate the other.'

Alan and Daphne charted Christopher's progress as closely as they could, and made sure they gathered as many details as possible, becoming more anxious than ever when they heard he had crossed into Italy where the Germans were putting up fierce resistance, immediately after the Italian forces had surrendered. Alan often proudly quoted his son's letters in his own correspondence to *The Times*, although he rarely named him. He passed on details from one of Christopher's letters that said:

Of all unjust things I think the most unjust is that the infantryman should be the lowest paid soldier in the British Army. His is by far the hardest job, and it is a job that is utterly different from his civil occupation. It doesn't seem fair that the mechanic who tinkered with tappets before the war, and who is now in Naples still happily tinkering with tappets, should be earning more than the farm labourer who is living in hole somewhere near Cassino.

162

CHAPTER FOURTEEN

Alan told his friends all he could about Christopher's movements. In July 1944 he was exchanging regular letters with Kenneth Grahame's wife Elspeth about her book *First Whispers of The Wind in the Willows*, which he agreed to review for *The Sunday Times*, one of very few book reviews he wrote during the war. He told her:

> *For the last two years he has been abroad. First to Irak [sic]: then three thousand miles across deserts to join the 8th Army at Enfidaville: then with the 5th Army for the first landing at Salerno: then Anzio: and then, after seven months continuous fighting in Italy, back to the Middle East: preparatory, I suppose, to some new landing somewhere. When last heard from he was bathing in the Sea of Galilee.*

When Alan heard about Christopher's visit to the Holy Land, he immediately dispatched two highly significant books, Ernest Renan's *The Life of Jesus* and *The Martyrdom of Man* by Winwood Reade. Both meant a great deal to Alan as they explored his own controversial belief that God had not created Man in his own image, but rather it had been the other way around and Man had actually created God.

By the time he received his father's parcel Christopher was in Italy and read the books lying in a tent 'somewhere on the narrow strip of sand that divides Lake Comacchio from the Adriatic'. The arguments fascinated Christopher, just as they had satisfied Alan many years before, and this new mutual sympathy and understanding became yet another bond that forged their relationship. Alan had always hoped that Christopher would come to share his religious opinions, although this was the first time he had made them clear. As a child Christopher was never christened, and was left to make his own mind up about the Church. Although Alan had been reluctant to force his views on Christopher until that point, he was delighted when the books made such an impact, answering many of his questions and doubts about God.

He had given the church twenty-four years' head start to convince Christopher, but it had failed: 'I read the letter many times,'

Christopher replied. 'It joined the others in my battledress pocket and was in its turn joined by yet others until the pocket bulged too much.'

This reticence over sharing his spiritual beliefs until Christopher was old enough to fully appreciate them was typical of Alan who always found it much easier to write than to talk to his son. Christopher's rather sad comment: 'My father remained buttoned up all his life,' showed how Alan could be seen as cold and taciturn, when actually he just preferred to keep his opinions to himself. And it was a trait Christopher shared, they both despised people who were overly open or loquacious, and tended to admire quiet modesty. One of Alan's favourite stories about modesty involved an elderly couple who found themselves at an English rural village fete, where the main attraction was an Indian snake charmer who passed out just as all the snakes slithered out of their box:

> It was then that the elderly wife, who we shall call Mary, came into her own, he wrote. She picked up the pipe and at the very moment that panic was beginning to spread among the spectators, as the masterless snakes started looking for amusement in the crowd, she sat cross-legged on the ground and began to play. The snakes heard the music and hurried back entranced. One by one she picked them up and returned them safely to their box. "Why, Mary darling," her husband said, "we have known each other for more than fifty years, and you never told me you could charm snakes!"
>
> And Mary said, "You never asked me, John."

In another of his letters to Elspeth Grahame, dated August 1944, Alan provided more details of Christopher's progress, in reply to a request she made for both of their autographs:

> Of course I send your blacksmith my autograph – hoping that he will have heard of me. As for C.R.'s that must wait until he makes a real claim on his own merits to a place in anybody's collection. It is on these lines that I have tried to bring him up:

CHAPTER FOURTEEN

I think successfully. At any rate, he was, and is, the most unassuming boy I have ever known. He has now gone back to Italy; and on the whole we are glad. He has been out of the war for four months, and his division was bound to go back into it soon, somewhere; and Italy takes him farther from – what every parent and wife dreads – the Far East.

Christopher had only been back in the relative safety of the Italian borders for a couple of months, on his second spell as a platoon commander with the Sappers, when his parents received the news they had dreaded for so long. On 7 October a telegram arrived from the War Office. It was brief and gave the stark announcement that Christopher Milne had been 'wounded' but did not give any further details about how serious the injuries were. 'Leaving it to the imagination to work on any horrible picture that rose to the mind,' Alan said. Three days later a second telegram followed, offering little to relieve their anxiety: 'The officer had suffered a penetrating shell wound in the right upper occipital region and was seriously ill,' was all it said.

Christopher was being treated for a head injury at the Advance Dressing Station on the Lombardy Plain in northwest Italy. The next day the matron of the hospital sent another letter but without adding much detail, simply confirming that he was 'seriously wounded'.

Alan was frantic with worry, and wrote to Chamberlain: 'We have had the hell of an anxious time, the news being conveyed by the W.O. in the most frightening way possible. I was unable to think of much else for some days.'

As it turned out, the wound was not as serious as they first feared. Christopher had a very lucky escape, and the day he arrived at hospital he was immediately operated on under local anaesthetic to remove pieces of broken bone from his head. He made a remarkably swift recovery and astounded Alan by writing just five days later: 'Surprisingly I rather enjoyed it. It was something entirely new, an experience and most interesting.' Alan was in awe of his son's remarkable attitude and wrote to Chamberlain that he was prouder than ever before: 'He has inherited a lot from me – but NOT THAT.'

It later emerged that Christopher could have written to his parents even earlier, had he known how worried they were, but did not realise that they had already been informed about the incident, and thought that they he was giving them the first news of his wound. He assured them there was absolutely nothing to worry about as he was expected to make a complete recovery and be fully fit within six short weeks.

The Milnes were hugely relieved by Christopher's comforting words, but also concerned by the suggestion that he would 'be back in the battle again in a few weeks'. Alan was still shocked by the offhand way that the War Office had passed on the news, and fired off a letter to *The Times*, without naming Christopher, making his views abundantly clear. Published on 28 October under the headline 'Casualty Notifications' it read:

> *If it is necessary, as it apparently is, to classify all head wounds as "serious", then it is all the more necessary that the Matron should fill in the picture and that her letter should be delayed until she has seen the casualty for herself and given him an opportunity, if he can avail himself of it, of sending a message home. I should like to add that the patient had nothing but gratitude for the kindness and sympathy shown him at the hospital. If a little imaginative sympathy were also shown for the next of kin it would save much unnecessary suffering.*

Luckily there would be no need for any more suffering as Christopher was not wounded again. But there was a different kind of heartbreak in store, for which Alan could not have prepared himself. In Trieste, where Christopher was stationed for his last few months in the army, he fell in love for the first time. She was a part Austrian, part Italian woman named Hedda who apparently taught him a great deal and started to loosen the bonds between Christopher and Alan.

Alan often said that his greatest wish was that Christopher should stand on his own two feet and make his own name for himself, but when it finally started to happen, Alan found it very hard to deal with. For the time being however, there was plenty to celebrate. Peace was declared in August 1945, and Adolf Hitler was dead. Christopher could return to Cotchford and complete his final year at Cambridge. For Alan that day could not come soon enough, but unfortunately it would be over a year before his battalion was demobilised, and he finally made it home the following August.

Alan was so cheerful at the prospect of Christopher's homecoming that he even managed to find something positive to say about what was arguably the worst horror of the war, the atomic bomb. Although he was still a pacifist at heart, on the day Japan surrendered to the Allied Forces, another of his letters appeared in *The Times*:

The object of war is to impose the national will upon another nation by the destruction of so much of its resources, human and material, that it cannot resist. Opinion has varied from time to time whether nations have a moral right to do this: a) in aggression on another country; b) to stop such aggression. The general opinion in England today is that a) is a crime against God and humanity, and that b) is a moral duty; a few people however, condemn both a) and b) with a kindly recommendation to mercy in the case of b).

It is absurd to suppose that an a) nation, which looks forward to cheerfully killing a million innocent people for the sake of some material end, is going to exhibit a nice humanity about its methods of murder; and it is insulting to suppose that a b) nation, which has reluctantly accepted an arbitrament repulsive to it, because it believes that there are higher values at stake than human lives, will risk the cause and deny its belief by making an exception in the case of the enemy's lives. If war is to be abolished, it will not be abolished by pretending that one method of killing is pleasing to God, and another displeasing; by accepting gratefully 200 raids with ordinary bombs which kill 1,000 "civilians" apiece, and exhibiting sanctimonious horror at one raid with an atomic bomb which kills the same number of "civilians" and spares 20,000 airmen's lives.

Every distinction between weapons of war as legitimate and illegitimate, as acceptable by or repugnant to humanity, is one more acknowledgement that was itself is acceptable and legitimate, so long as it is conducted, not in the latest fashion, but in the latest fashion but one.

War will cease when statesmen are intelligent enough to realise what the man in the street has known for a long time, that it is a wicked game and a fool's game. The atomic bomb brings this moment nearer; not because it adds to the wickedness of war, for nothing could do that, but because it makes plain, even to the sub-human intelligence, the folly of it.

CHAPTER FIFTEEN

'Promise me you'll never forget me because if I thought you would I'd never leave.'

As soon as peace was declared across Europe, and party politics resumed once again, Winston Churchill, the Prime Minister who had led the Allied Forces to victory suddenly found himself redundant. Military victory had been his sole purpose for the past five years, and without a clear sense of purpose or direction he lost the General Election. Many people voted Labour for the first time, leading to a landslide victory for Clement Atlee in July 1945, but Alan bucked the trend and voted Conservative for the first time in his life.

Alan was still left wing in his political views, and longed for social reform, but he feared the Labour Party's sympathy for Russia and hated the idea that their plans for nationalisation and public ownership might lead to a new form of communism. He also resented a tendency at the time to refer to communism as 'socialism', which he saw as an attempt 'to cover up the essential tyranny of communism'.

Alan found the entire political landscape utterly depressing, and was afraid that the seeds were already being sown for yet another global conflict as Stalin refused the call for free elections and democracy in Eastern Europe, and the Iron Curtain fell heavily again. In a poem called *Passed to the News Chronicle for Confirmation*, he wrote:

> *I doubt if we have ever had*
> *A world so sad and mad and bad,*
> *And being part of it, I see*
> *That part of it is due to me.*

He agonised over his decision to vote Conservative, breaking the habit of a lifetime, having always had a strongly entrenched sense of revulsion for the right-wing party. Alan still considered himself Liberal at heart but felt badly let down by the new policies. He felt disappointed that the party had almost no chance of making any impression on the worrying situation, as they seemed far too tolerant of the totalitarian ideals in Moscow for his liking:

Liberals have much to remember and much to forgive, he wrote to *The Times. I doubt if there has ever been a more contemptible exhibition of bad manners, bad sportsmanship and selfish stupidity than was given by the self-styled Gentlemanly Party during those years of Liberal ascendancy. Mr Churchill would probably agree. Many Liberals are still living in those far-off days. In the manner of Dr Johnson, they say to every Conservative candidate, "Sir, I perceive you are a vile Tory"; when they see a Tory they "see a rascal". Even if they had to choose between a Conservative and a Communist, they would choose the Communist, fooling themselves, as they have fooled themselves over every Communist-inspired party abroad, into the belief that the farther you move to the "left", the less like a reactionary Tory you become.*

Many years ago I defined a true Liberal (meaning myself, of course) as one who hated Fascism and Communism equally. How many Liberals are to be found now in the Liberal Party? Very few.

And in a later letter he added to his views, saying:

For myself I do not think that peace depends on the alleged love of peace of this or that Prime Minister; but it does depend on their respective policies. The two main buttresses of the peaceful world which we all want to build are a united Western Europe and an unbreakable friendship between England and America.

CHAPTER FIFTEEN

While the aftershocks of the war left the political landscape altered forever, much had stayed the same at Cotchford Farm. The family housekeeper Mrs Wilson may have been a force to be reckoned with who made undrinkable coffee – and it was very important never to upset her – yet she remained unswervingly loyal through years of uncertainty, battling every day with the farm's temperamental generator. On V.E. Day Alan sent her a gift, expressing his appreciation: 'To dear Mrs Wilson, a token of our Gratitude for all she has done for us during the war: not forgetting the delightful time she has had with the Engine. From A.A. Milne.' The gardener George Tasker also stayed devoted to the family during war and peace, tending to Daphne's beloved dahlia and chrysanthemums, and somehow managing to supplement their dreary restricted diet with a variety of vegetables. They were all tremendously relieved when peace was restored, but after dangerously near misses from two flying bombs the house was plagued with new cracks and draughts. There was no further need for blackouts each night, and when the Home Guard was dissolved, Alan could finally give up his early morning struggles to start his car. He had bought the motor in 1935 and was desperate for a new one, which he ordered immediately after the war, although for some reason it was not delivered until 1952. Slowly life began to return to normal.

In the weeks following the declaration of peace, while he waited as patiently as he could for his son to return, Leonard Russell of *The Sunday Times* sent Alan a new book to review. It was an autobiography by Nancy Spain, a young writer who joined the Women's Royal Navy Service during the war and wrote about her experiences as she travelled around the country recruiting young female officers. Alan was horrified that a woman should have been given such a role, and according to Daphne, when he opened the parcel he furiously threw the book across the room shouting: 'A war book, by a girl!' Daphne calmly retrieved it and read the book herself, before urging her husband to read it too, telling him: 'It's all about nothing'.

Alan took his wife's sensible advice, not for the first time, and his review of *Thank You Nelson* soon appeared in the newspaper under the headline *A Wren's Eye View of the Proper Navy*. It caused a sensation and made Nancy Spain's name, so she was sure to thank Alan personally for his review when she went on to become one of the most senior reporters at the *Daily Express*: 'That review of A.A. Milne's sold out the whole of the first edition and the whole of the second,' she said. 'Indeed, I knew the book must be a success when the Chief Officer Administration at WRNS headquarters said, "The book was disappointing after the review."' Spain was amazed when Alan replied, inviting her to lunch at Cotchford:

> *You will have to work up an enthusiasm for gardens first, he warned her. Nothing annoys my wife (and me too) so much as seeing a visitor step heavily back on to a clump of aubrietia behind her, ignore the tulips in front of her, and ask if we have been to many theatres lately.*

Understandably nervous about what sort of welcome she could expect from the Milnes, she bravely took the train down from Victoria station, and arrived in plenty of time to dutifully admire the gardens before lunch. Years later she still remembered every detail of the delicious meal: 'Hot boiled salmon, peas, new potatoes, asparagus, strawberries and cream. A real cricketer's, schoolboy's or schoolgirl's lunch. There is no better lunch in the world,' she said. Nancy went on to paint a vivid portrait of life at the farm, revealing how utterly devoted to each other Daphne and Alan appeared to be, despite the rumours and gossip which swirled about the unusual amount of time they had spent apart before the war:

> *It was a glorious summer's day and the Milnes were perfectly right about their garden. All the flowers had come triumphantly into bloom at the same instant: and there was an enormous pink tree like a feather duster over the front door. It looked as though it had been worked in cross-stitch on a tea cosy until you came closer and saw that the whole thing was real. A.A. Milne and his wife were adorable too,* Nancy

recalled. She called him Blue and *certainly he had the bluest eyes I have ever seen in a human being. Matching up to them were his blazer, that summer sky, his socks, his handkerchief and quite large patches of the garden.*

And everywhere there were relics of Winnie-the-Pooh. Daphne Milne told me that there was a first edition of The House at Pooh Corner *under the sundial and we drank sherry poured out of a large blown glass orange reproduction of Piglet. The sherry came out of its mouth.*

A.A. Milne was a first class companion. He talked a lot about the importance of light verse and what an excellent thing it was for discipline to drop into it from time to time. "Light verse writing makyth a very exact man." He said that the important thing in writing was to keep "oneself" out of the way of the reader. "Otherwise the perspiration shows." And he said that the telephone was a monstrous intrusion on privacy. At the time I was more than a little shocked by this, but now that my telephone rings frequently I know what he meant.

C.S. Calverley was the chap to imitate, he said. Calverley, who wrote Fly Leaves and Verses and Translations. *Thank goodness I had the instinct to keep my mouth shut, and the sense to ask him for the titles of the books. When I got back to London I even went gravely to the British Museum and read them.*

He went on mildly talking, this enchanting blue-eyed man, all that precious summer's afternoon, distilling the wisdom of years into a casual conversation. "Any creative writer's criticism of another is no more than a statement of the obvious truth that he would have written the book differently himself," he told me. "All writers write to please themselves," he said. "No sensible author wants anything but praise."

As is clear from this description of Alan's idyllic life, he hardly needed to work anymore, and could have eased himself into a gentle retirement, yet when his new novel *Chloe Marr* was published in 1946, he was livid that the critics still persisted with references to *Winnie-*

the-Pooh, more two decades after he had written them. He thought he had left all that in the past, but the children's books were doing better than ever, and there was no escaping them, or their effect on his reputation.

When Irish dramatist St John Ervine wrote to congratulate Alan on *Chloe Marr*, saying how much he enjoyed it, Alan replied:

> *Whenever a critic begins his notice with a reference to Winnie-the-Pooh, I know that, not only will he be insulting but that he decided to be so before he read the book. Which saves him the trouble of reading it. Yours is the letter of a real friend and (may I add immodestly?) an obviously super-intelligent critic.*

Alan had been working on *Chloe Marr* for more than five years, despite Chamberlain giving him frequent nudges to complete the manuscript. When it eventually emerged it was his first novel to be published by Methuen in thirteen years. It would also be his last. But it turned out to be a considerable success, selling 16,415 copies in Britain in its first six months alone, and in America the initial print run of 30,000 copies sold out too. Across the Atlantic the reviews were generally more favourable: 'The Old Enchanter has done it again,' gushed one newspaper. It was certainly very different from anything Alan had written in the past, telling the story of a young and beautiful woman adored by various besotted men in London society. Much speculation surrounded the elusive character of Chloe, as each of her friends in turn discovered something new to unlock her mysterious past. Seen entirely through the eyes of her devoted admirers, in the end, without explaining what is going on in her mind, she died in a plane crash.

The *Times Literary Supplement* declared that Alan had 'gone modern' by exploring 'the grief and happiness, hopes and fears of the ordinary people', while *The Sunday Times* decided it was 'high entertainment with an almost constant sparkle'. On the whole there was a great deal of praise for the charming characters and scintillating dialogue which peppered the book, although many of the reviews did mention *Pooh*, and Alan's most dreaded word 'whimsical' popped up far too many times for his liking. And when he was interviewed by the *Evening News* to mark the publication of *Chloe Marr*, the paper was more interested in reporting the latest news of Christopher:

> *Lieut. Christopher Robin Milne, whose fortunes have kept pace with the generation that fought this war, is now recovered from the wound he got in the fighting in Italy. "No I don't know what he will take up yet," said Mr Milne, just like hundreds of fathers. "He may write, but it is a difficult time for young writers. Look at the size of your paper."*

What Alan meant was that when he started his career as a young journalist there were eight evening papers in London alone, all of which would willingly print articles from unknown freelancers, which he calculated gave him: 'Forty-eight chances each week of a guinea, to say nothing of the obese morning papers. Now the outlook for the young is become bleak indeed.' At the age of 26, Christopher had no plans beyond finishing his degree. Shortly after he arrived home in the summer of 1946, Alan wrote to St John Ervine: 'Our boy is with us, and gets demobilised next week; after which he goes back to Cambridge for a year, chiefly to give the world a little time in which to cool.'

Beyond his obvious joy at having Christopher home safely, Alan was starting to find much of life a chore. While he was not quite a recluse, he found himself turning down more and more invitations as making the journey to London and back even once a week was taking its toll. For years he had been traveling up to the capital on a Tuesday, mostly for lunches at The Garrick Club, but now committing to anything more on top of that was out of the question. Making his apologies to a meeting of the Royal Literary Fund he explained:

> *I'm afraid I shan't be coming up for the Literary Fund meeting on Wednesday, so cannot accept your kind invite. I go up on Tuesday every week anyway – of necessity – and on this particular week I am "judging" at a RADA show at the Lyric*

on Thursday. To make the stop-at-every-station journey to London and back three days running (or rather stopping) is too much for me. It can't be done, alas; but thank you so much for suggesting it.

His friends started to notice that he was becoming increasingly cold and unfriendly as old age began to creep up on him. Publisher Rupert Hart-Davis remembered seeing Alan in the Garrick but finding him 'gloomy and aloof,' while *Punch* writer Basil Boothroyd thought of him as 'an austere and somewhat tetchy figure, in contrast with his charming literary style'. His sour demeanour came largely from the dawning realisation that he was starting to lose his close bond with Christopher. In *Chloe Marr* he wrote tellingly about a boy killed by a car when he was a child, and years after the accident his father reflected:

Jonathan, if he had lived, would have been grown up by this time; any expressions of love between them would have been bad form, even if there was love left to express. They would meet rarely, write as little as possible. He would dislike his daughter-in-law, or she him. Father and son would differ in politics, in tastes, in creed. There were so many barriers to unity. You love your children; you will never stop loving them. That's the only love which never changes, never dies.

Alan knew this change was inevitable. Back in 1931 he had told an interviewer: 'If I make a success of Christopher Robin as a person I will consider it my greatest creative work,' and he appeared to have achieved his aim. Christopher was not only highly intelligent, but also thoughtful and caring. Alan praised him lavishly at any opportunity, and like Alan, Christopher still loved literature, music, and nature, but he was starting to realise that he could only really be himself by escaping his father's influence, and his celebrated childhood. They were both starting to understand that the only way for him to flourish now would be to sacrifice his close relationship with Alan.

CHAPTER FIFTEEN

After completing his final eight months at Cambridge, and graduating with a poor third-class degree in English Literature, the only thing that looked certain about Christopher's future was that he would face a tough time out in the real world, which Alan had tried so hard to protect him from for so long. He talked vaguely about following his father's footsteps into writing, or perhaps trying to land a job in the publishing industry, or maybe he would like to make furniture. He tried job after job, without success. He attempted to write light articles, just as Alan had done forty years earlier, but almost all of them were sent back to him and never published. He contacted the Central Office of Information – the new name of the Ministry that Alan had written for during the war – but they had nothing for him either. Then, on a completely different tack, he landed a position as a trainee furniture buyer with the John Lewis Partnership, but when he failed to turn up in an appropriate business suit they sacked him. The same quiet modesty Alan had always praised was now making it difficult for Christopher to push himself forward, and he had to accept that he would never be quite like his father.

Although he resented his father's interference in the past, now Christopher blamed Alan for not doing more to help him, given the fact that he was the one to thank for his vast success, wealth and fame:

I was the wrong person in the wrong place with qualifications nobody wanted, Christopher said. Other fathers were reaching down with helping hand to their sons. But what was mine doing? What, to be fair, could mine do? He had made his own way by his own efforts, and had left behind him no path that could be followed. But were they entirely his own efforts? Hadn't I come into it somewhere? In pessimistic moments, when I was trudging London in search of an employer wanting to make use of such talents as I could offer, it seemed to me, almost, that my father had got to where he was by climbing on my infant shoulders, that he had filched from me my good name and left me with the empty fame of being his son.

This was the worst period for me. It was a period when, suitably encouraged, my bitterness would overflow.

It was in those particularly difficult months in 1947, when he was unemployed following his graduation from university, that their relationship really broke down:

At home I was only jealous of my father when he beat me at golf. The rest of the time we were not rivals but friends. The sun shone equally on us both. Neither stood in the other's shadow. But in 1947 all this changed, Christopher reflected. *Up to then we had run neck and neck. He had been the better cricketer but I had been the better mathematician. We had both done equally badly at Cambridge, but I – with a six-year break for the war – could offer the better excuse. We had both been equally indifferent soldiers, but I had at least started from the ranks; and a wound in the head was surely more glorious than trench fever. We had been companions but now our ways were to part.*

The two Milne men may perhaps have still had more in common than they realised, but as was typical of the time neither of them was prepared to reveal their emotions or talk openly about it. Christopher wrote in his autobiography:

Neither of us knew what the other thought. We could only guess. Did he guess right? Did he sympathise? Was he resentful? Did he have any feelings of guilt? Well, he had his own battles to fight, and curiously, they were not dissimilar from mine. If I was jealous of him, he was no less jealous of himself. If I wanted to escape from Christopher Robin, so too did he.

After the war he turned to short stories. He had always written what he wanted to write. His luck was that this was also what the public wanted to read. Now his luck was deserting him. People didn't want books of short stories. Nor did they want long philosophical poems. Not even collections of random reflections.

CHAPTER FIFTEEN

He at the top of the hill, I at the bottom: we each had our sorrows, our moments of disillusion. We were both of us unwanted.

The following year, Christopher spent a week's holiday with his parents back at his childhood home in Sussex, but the atmosphere was tense and awkward. He had just called off his engagement to the girl he fell in love with in Trieste, and the long-distance passionate romance had left him a changed man. He was living alone in a small flat in London, and Daphne's father's second wife Nancy suggested he to get to know his cousin who was also living in the city at the time. Lesley de Selincourt was the daughter of Daphne's brother Aubrey, the estranged brother she had not spoken to in more than twenty-five years following their feud over borrowed money that was never returned. Daphne and Aubrey's father had initially opposed his marriage to a woman called Irene, Lesley's mother, but the intervening years had proved him wrong. The couple taught together at a school in Shanklin on the Isle of Wight, and former pupils later told how Aubrey and Irene transformed their lives with vivid readings of Shakespeare and *Moby Dick*, and one girl said they had shown her that, 'It was possible for middle-aged married people still to be in love with each other.'

Christopher was introduced to his cousin on 5 February 1948 and on 31 March, during a visit home, he stunned his parents by announcing that they had fallen in love:

This is about the limit of Moon's conversation right now. He is (apparently) in love again and "thinking of 'er" all the time, Alan wrote in one of his regular letters to Ken's widow Maud. *We see little of him save at meals, and get nothing from him then except an affirmative, negative or non-committal grunt (it is difficult to distinguish between them) in answer to a direct question. He came down on Saturday night and goes back on Saturday morning; I had no idea before that there were so many meals in a week. Daff is in London today, so I have had to do all the work myself. Luckily she will be back to dinner; she is more dauntless than I am, and got a couple of forced laughs out of him the other day. All very trying, but I suppose it will pass.*

Alan was describing a scene that may be familiar to many parents of adolescents, but Christopher was in fact 27 years old, and had actually been a charming teenager. Now, having met Lesley, he appeared to ready to make a complete break away from his parents, albeit belatedly, and years later he reflected about that deeply uncomfortable period in his memoirs: 'Children drift away from their parents as they grow up, and it is right that they should. I had been very close to mine, especially to my father, for rather longer than is usual, and so the drifting when it came was perhaps a little further than usual.'

Alan and Daphne also lost their pet golden cocker spaniel that year, and were both utterly bereft, but finding themselves unexpectedly thrown together in such emotional turmoil for the first time in many years seemed to bring them closer than ever. The dog was buried under silver birch trees in the wood which the Milnes had planted themselves between the house and the Maresfield Road. And years later, after Alan's death, Daphne shocked her household staff by issuing instructions for a sculpture of Christopher's head to be buried under the same trees, where she would never have to lay eyes on it again.

The rift between Christopher and his parents was hugely exacerbated by the fact that the woman he was determined to marry was Daphne's niece. Alan was deeply concerned about the potential genetic implications for any future children they might have, and he could not help hating that, on top of everything else, Lesley was Aubrey's daughter. He still despised Daphne's wayward brother who constantly demanded loans that were never repaid. And, as if all that were not bad enough, Lesley made it quite clear that she despised *Winnie-the-Pooh*. While the rest of the world was blissfully enchanted by the tales, the woman who fell in love with the real Christopher Robin felt nothing but resentment for what the stories had done to the man.

CHAPTER FIFTEEN

The two most important women in Christopher's life had absolutely nothing in common, Lesley and Daphne were both equally amazed that they were so closely related. Most people were horrified when they discovered that Lesley's mother-in-law was also her aunt, but the lovebirds appeared not to care about the controversy, nor what it might mean for their children, and married on 24 July 1948 at Holy Trinity Church in West London. Somehow Alan and Daphne forced themselves to make an appearance at the wedding against their better judgment, as did Aubrey, and Ken's son Tony was the best man. *The Times* recorded the low-key affair: 'The bride, who was given away by her father, wore a crinoline gown of white net and taffeta, and was attended by two child bridesmaids, Anne-Marie de Selincourt and Alison Murray-Rust. Mr Antony Milne was best man.'

Arriving at the church at 4pm, with the eyes of the media watching, it was the first time Alan and Daphne had seen her estranged brother in a quarter of a century. Everybody put on polite smiles for the occasion, but there was no suggestion that this bizarre union would do anything to help bury their differences or restore peace to the family. Following the ceremony, there was a small and somewhat strained reception at Brown's Hotel, which had become Alan's favourite place to stay in London now that they no longer owned the house in Chelsea.

After the ordeal was over, Alan retreated to his Sussex sanctuary and was rarely seen in London again. He occupied himself by writing short stories, including *The Rise and Fall of Mortimer Scrivens*, an amusing warning to anyone who borrows books and fails to return them. He also branched out into murder mysteries, and gave himself the challenge of tackling several stories in a female voice. Without Christopher to distract him now, Alan was producing stories at a prolific rate, and he explained the process to his agent:

As I have written thirty plays, long or short, there are usually plenty of these. The resulting manuscript is so crossed out, rubbed out, interlined or generally messed up, as to be indecipherable by anybody else, and sometimes by me. I write

*it all out again in ink (this is rather a bore) and send it away to
be typed. This gives me ten days before it comes back; during
which I can tell myself that I am still in the middle of that
particular story, and may do nothing with an easy conscience.*

He found that doing nothing came more easily in the summer months,
with his great passions for gardening and cricket, but in the winter he
tended to focus even more on his work than ever, hiding himself away
in his study for hours on end.

His notoriety meant Alan never had the slightest difficulty getting
his stories published, but they did not sell well. They appeared in a
wide variety of magazines including *Cosmopolitan, Good
Housekeeping* and *Modern Women*, and there were two collections
issued by Dutton's – *Birthday Party* in 1948 and *A Table Near the
Band* in 1950 – but sales figures for both books were very low. He
found his dwindling popularity depressing and turned down the trickle
of invitations he received, although he still made the effort to stay in
touch with Anne Darlington who had inspired him to write the very
first *Pooh* poems all those years ago. He sent her a copy of *A Table
Near The Band* for Christmas 1950, with the message: 'But for whom
the first story would never have been written, and the Milnes would
have missed a lot of happiness and laughter – with more than twenty-
five years love from Blue.' Anne's husband Peter Ryde recalled a rare
occasion when Alan did accept one of her dinner invitations, and Anne
rushed around polishing everything in the house, and served him a
lavish meal of oysters and champagne. But he said Alan, while usually
charming and pleasant, made very little effort to be entertaining and
sat 'almost as if barricaded within himself'.

Alan's reputation as an adult author was in serious decline in
America as well, and he would not take any comfort from the fact that
the children's books continued to fly off the shelves. Elliot Macrae at
Dutton's had the difficult job of breaking the news that Alan's name
was not enough to sell his new adult books and a large-scale plan to
promote them proved a complete failure. The publisher's original
intention to print 600,000 copies was halved at the last minute, and

even then they lost a fortune on unsold books and he said they ended up 'stuck with two hundred and twenty thousand assorted titles'.

It was not much consolation, but many of Alan's old plays were still being performed around Britain and abroad. In 1948 alone thirteen different plays were produced, *The Dover Road* was staged twelve times, and the ever popular *Mr Pim Passes By* was put on at no less than sixteen theatres. The royalty cheques poured in, but the vast proportion of Alan's enormous income would always come from the *Winnie-the-Pooh* stories and poems. Whether he liked it or not – and he maintained that he did not – his bank account bulged with deposits from worldwide translations and their subsidiary rights, not to mention the unprecedented sales of toys, games and records. His personal share of the American merchandise sales alone in 1947 was over $2,000, so he could hardly complain; plus he knew that the children's books gave him the freedom to write whatever he pleased without having to worry about sales or marketing. But he even found that the pleasure he used to get from writing was starting to wear thin: 'To a writer one day is very much like another day. He gets up, he eats, he writes, he eats, he thinks, he potters, he eats, he writes, he eats, he reads, he goes to bed,' he explained. And he was feeling so low about the quality of his work, that he even went so far as to suggest that his pet cat Cleopatra's kittens were much more impressive: 'Hers is a great achievement,' he wrote. 'What is one short story to four delightful kittens?'

Over time Alan abandoned his small study on the ground floor and preferred to stay hidden away in his bedroom on the first floor as it had large windows on two sides, overlooking the glorious garden below. In 1950 he was photographed at his desk, showing yellow floral curtains and a bright Indian rug on the floor. Elliot Macrae flew over from New York to visit Alan at home and when he went upstairs, could not help but notice Christopher's old toys looking as dejected and fed up with life as Alan himself. He asked if he could borrow Pooh, Piglet, Tigger, Kanga, and Eeyore, and whisked them away for a triumphant tour of America. Roo was missing, having been lost by Christopher years ago in the apple orchard, and Piglet's face was a funny shape where a dog had bitten him. Alan issued each stuffed animal with a handwritten 'birth certificate' giving their fictitious histories, and on arrival in New York, they were insured for the princely sum of $50,000 before travelling around the country for several years, visiting libraries and department stores, schools and offices. Fans would travel through all kinds of weather and wait for hours just to catch a glimpse of Pooh and his chums.

> *Everywhere Pooh went we had a guest book for people to sign. We sent the books to Milne so he could see their comments, like "We love Pooh" and "I travelled two hundred miles just to see Pooh". He seemed to enjoy those and decided Dutton's should keep the animals. We like to say that Pooh became an American citizen,*

Elliot Graham, the publicity director at Dutton's recalled.

Luckily Christopher was not remotely bothered that his father had taken his old toys from the nursery and given then away without consulting him first. He dismissed them saying:

> *If you saw them today, your immediate reaction would be: "How old and battered and lifeless they look." But of course they are old and battered and lifeless. They are only toys and you are mistaking them for the real animals who lived in the forest.*

And he added:

> *I like to have around me the things I like today, not the things I once liked many years ago. I don't want a house to be a museum.*
>
> *Every child has his Pooh, but one would think it odd if every man still kept his Pooh to remind him of childhood. My toys were and are no more than yours were and are to you. I do not love them more because they are known to children in Australia or Japan. Fame has nothing to do with love.*

CHAPTER FIFTEEN

Alan's one condition, as he handed his son's childhood toys over, was that they should never be cleaned and always look as if a child had only just finished playing with them: 'No explanation is needed for the world-weariness of Pooh and Eeyore,' he wrote. 'Time's hand has been upon them since 1921. That was a long time ago.'

Alan was finding it harder to conceal his own sense of world-weariness too. When his great-niece Alison begged him to send her some poetry at Godolphin School in Salisbury he obliged, and also sent autographs for her friends. But the verses, using the Latin term for crustaceans, seemed rather bleak for a schoolgirl to receive:

> *I'm weary of this world of strife.*
> *I'd like to have a stab*
> *At living the untroubled life*
> *Of (say) a hermit crab.*
> *No word of bombs, of A or H,*
> *Has ever crossed his lips.*
> *None talk to him of Shin or Strach.*
> *He's deaf to news of Cripps.*
> *His pools are not the football pools,*
> *Nor sea the B.B.C.*
> *No letters from dolphin schools*
> *Demanding poetry.*
> *What if imagination lends*
> *Enchantment to the view?*
> *Entomostraca! (George to friends)*
> *I would that I were you!*

CHAPTER SIXTEEN

'How lucky I am to have something that makes saying goodbye so hard.'

After he married Lesley, Alan barely saw Christopher again, and the wound that opened up between them made him examine and question everything around him, even his strongly held religious beliefs. Years earlier he and Christopher had bonded when Alan sent him a copy of *The Martyrdom Of Man* when he was fighting in the war. Now, he prepared to be branded a heretic and a blasphemer with the publication of *The Norman Church*, which Christopher later referred to as 'a long philosophical poem'.

Sadly for Alan, few people cared enough to even attack him. His views were dismissed as unsurprising, and the book was never published in America where he certainly had legions of fans. But he did not propose any new ideas, he simply reiterated a belief he had expressed before, that the two testaments of the Bible were in such violent opposition that it was ridiculous to suggest they could both be part of the same religion. He attempted to make a clear distinction between what he called 'the objective God, of whom we can only say with certainty that he is the Creative Spirit or First Cause, and the subjective man-imagined God'. He included all the contradictory incarnations – including the Pope's Catholic God, Mohammed's God and St Paul's God – which he said must be set up by man. He added that he wanted nothing at all to do with a God that decreed that:

> *Babies dying unbaptized*
> *Were damned in Hell. Was God surprised*
> *To hear that this was what Himself had authorized?*

CHAPTER SIXTEEN

The book may have made very little impression on the wider world, but in the Milne's rural village of Hartfield it confirmed what many people in the close-knit Christian community already thought, that the couple were atheists and sinners. It did not help that Daphne was always very generous about giving away flowers from their garden, as long as they were not going to the church. They already had a reputation for their superior attitude, and several locals took further offence at an unexpectedly humorous passage in the lengthy poem, which suggested that Alan knew what was going on in their heads during Sunday church services:

> *The choir-boys shuffle in their seats;*
> *A housewife mentally completes*
> *Tomorrow's washing list; her lord*
> *Adds up the hymns upon the board.*
> *The Squire, as far as one can see,*
> *Is interested in a bee;*
> *A widow, reverently prim,*
> *Is wondering how best to slim-*
> *And all the maidens listen rapt, and "think of him".*

Then came another blow. In 1951 Christopher and Lesley announced that they were moving out to the West Country, leaving London to open a bookshop more than two hundred miles away in Dartmouth on the Devon coast, adding a huge geographical distance to the emotional gap they already had between them. Christopher said Daphne was baffled when she heard the news:

> *"I would have thought," said my mother, who always hit the nail on the head no matter whose fingers were in the way, "I would have thought that this was the one thing you would have absolutely hated. I thought you didn't like 'business'. You certainly didn't get on at John Lewis. And you're going to have to meet Pooh fans all the time. Really it does seem a very odd decision."*

Christopher and Lesley ran The Harbour Bookshop for many years with some success, refusing to accept any help from his father. And even though they dedicated very little shelf space to the four *Pooh* books, as they wanted the shop to succeed purely on its own merits, the place was always known fondly to locals and tourists as 'The Christopher Robin Bookshop'.

'Here was something my wife and I could do together as partners,' Christopher said. 'Here was something we could do in a part of England of our own choosing; and if I wasn't too happy about four of the books, there were still plenty of others.'

Despite his attempts to make a fresh start, the shop was constantly visited by fans hoping for a glimpse of the real Christopher Robin, which filled him 'with acute embarrassment'. Often people expected to find the little boy in the drawings:

Every year brings a new batch of readers, he explained. *Meeting Christopher Robin and Pooh for the first time, learning that maybe Christopher Robin is a real live person and expecting him to still look like his picture. Even if you are wise enough to realise that the books were written a long time ago and that real live people grow up, you may still find yourself judging them by today's standards. My father was writing in the 1920s about the 1920s to entertain people living in the 1920s and these were the attitudes current at the time.*

After Christopher retired, the premises became the Dartmouth Community Bookshop, a not-for-profit co-operative, and Christopher started work on three autobiographical books about his childhood and the myriad problems he felt his father's stories had caused him.

In January 1952 Alan turned 70, even though he had no interest in celebrating a milestone birthday. He echoed his own feelings some years earlier when Eeyore asked gloomily: 'What are birthdays? Here today and gone tomorrow.' He could still vividly remember a strange feeling of anticipation about ageing that he experienced as a small boy when he was having his hair brushed in a photographer's studio before posing for family portraits: 'One day I shall be old and it won't matter how long she took over my hair, because I shall be old, and it will all be over,' he had thought to himself at the time. Reaching 70 gave Alan pause for thought and he wrote:

It is indeed an extraordinary age to be: an age at which, without conscious effort, one should be clothed with dignity and authority; and here am I, invested with neither. However long a writer has been in the business, he is still without authority for anybody but himself. All he knows is how to write in his own way.

The day itself passed quietly, and as he later explained to Alison who was now in her last year at school, the main event had been the delivery of a crate of Scotch whisky even though it was well known that he absolutely hated the stuff: 'I had a very nice birthday,' he wrote in one of his regular letters.

My American publishers sent me twelve bottles of whiskey. Can you believe it? Compare this with the picture postcard which my English publishers didn't send me, and where are you? And a neighbour, whom we have only met once or twice and who had seen a paragraph in the Evening News congratulating me on being ninety, came round with a large pot of daffodils. As Wordsworth said:

> *And then my heart with pleasure fills*
> *And dances with the daffodils,*
> *Becoming pardonably frisky*
> *When filled as well with all this whisky.*

Retirement never crossed his mind, and in June that year Alan published his final book, *Year In, Year Out*. Christopher called it 'a collection of random reflections'. The critics were kind to Alan, to his great relief. Virginia Graham, reviewing it for the *Spectator* praised it as 'immaculate and sweet, but not excessively sentimental'. The *Times Literary Supplement* said: 'The book demonstrates Milne's erudition, wit and liberalism.'

But it was the review in *The Times* that pleased him most of all. Calling him 'damnably uncivic' and 'an unworthy president of the local horticultural society,' it went on:

> *Yet he can be an alarmingly good citizen, as when he writes to the paper on such tremendous subjects as income tax or the atomic bomb. In fact he can write delightfully, amusingly, ironically, and now and again almost ferociously on all manner of subjects. He provides a dish of fine, confused eating, offering a wide choice for the reader's money.*

Critics were equally effusive in America too, *The New York Times* said: 'Milne discusses a hundred or so everyday subjects, but is delightfully surprising, witty and graceful.'

Having his book so well received cheered Alan up enormously, so much so that he actually found himself looking back fondly on *Pooh* for the first time in decades. Feeling genial, he even broke the habit of a lifetime and wrote back to a young journalist from Cornwall who enjoyed reading *Year In, Year Out*. His reply was surprising, given how dour he had been about *Pooh* over the years:

> *I can't remember a letter which has given me as much pleasure as yours, he glowed. As your own fan-mail increases (as I am sure it will, for it is obvious that you can write), you will find that intelligent praise is the one stimulant which a writer needs. You will also find that, however proud he may be of earlier work, it is praise of his latest book which he appreciates most. So thank you for what you say of* Year In, Year Out*; as you can imagine, I enjoyed writing it – which is the only way I know of firing enjoyment in others. But you are right about Pooh. There was an intermediate period when any reference to him was infuriating; but now such a 'nice, comfortable feeling'*

envelops him that I can almost regard him impersonally as the creation of one of my favourite authors.

This marked a period of deep contemplation for Alan who again cast his mind back to Christopher's childhood when he was asked to write the preface for a special edition of his verses:

In real life very young children have an artless beauty, an innocent grace, an unstudied abandon of movement, which, taken together, make an appeal to our emotions similar in kind to that made by any other young artless creatures: kittens, puppies, lambs: but greater in degree, for the reason that the beauty of childhood seems in some way to transcend the body.

But with this outstanding physical quality there is a natural lack of moral quality, which expresses itself, as Nature always insists on expressing herself, in an egotism entirely ruthless.

And, by way of an explanation for his famous poem *James James Morrison Morrison*, which was always thought to be inspired by Daphne's frivolous shopping trips and long absences, Alan revealed that the pain of Christopher distancing himself from them had not healed:

The mother of a little boy of three has disappeared, and is never seen again. The child's reaction to the total loss of his mother is given in these lines:

> *James James*
> *Morrison Morrison*
> *(Commonly known as Jim)*
> *Told his*
> *Other relations*
> *Not to go blaming him.*

And that is all. It is the truth about a child: children are, indeed as heartless as that.

He agonised over Christopher, but Alan was definitely mellowing in his old age, which became clear when the *New York Herald Tribune* asked him to write something about his life at Cotchford to celebrate the new book's publication in the States, and he raised eyebrows once again by having yet more warm things to say about *Winnie-the-Pooh*. In a poem reflecting back over his long career he wrote:

> *If a writer, why not write*
> *On whatever comes in sight?*
> *So – the Children's Books: a short*
> *Intermezzo of a sort;*
> *When I wrote them, little thinking*
> *All my years of pen-and-inking*
> *Would be almost lost among*
> *Those four trifles for the young.*
> *Though a writer must confess his*
> *Works aren't all of them successes,*
> *Though his sermons fail to please,*
> *Though his humour no one sees,*
> *Yet he cannot help delighting*
> *In the pleasure of the writing*
> *In a farmhouse old by centuries*
> *This so happy an adventure is*
> *Coming (so I must suppose,*
> *Now I'm 70) to a close.*
> *Take it all, year in year out,*
> *I've enjoyed it, not a doubt.*

Those eerily predictive words made up the last poem Alan ever composed. Just three days later, on 15 October, Daphne wrote to Maud in what appears to be tear-stained red ink:

Share most terrible news. My darling Alan is very seriously ill and was taken last night to East Grinstead Hospital in an ambulance. He had a stroke.

CHAPTER SIXTEEN

I have just come back from the Hospital and he is expected
to live two or three days perhaps. It was so frightfully sudden.
I still find it impossible to believe.
My love to you, Daff.

The situation was dire but Alan's doctors got their predictions about his life expectancy quite wrong, and he went on to live for another three years and three months, although he never made a full recovery and remained an invalid. On 27 October, still dangerously ill but well enough to be moved, he was taken from East Grinstead to the Middlesex Hospital in London for further treatment. He was there when news broke that libraries all over Hungary had taken the extraordinary step of withdrawing all his books. Censors destroyed thousands of books by authors including Conan Doyle, Lewis Carroll, and Daphne du Maurier under the direct orders of Stalin. Alan was in no fit state to object.

And then in November, while Alan was still in hospital building his strength up for life-threatening surgery, Christopher took the unexpected step of agreeing to a rare interview with a reporter from the *Sunday Dispatch*. His harsh words, coming at such a difficult time, destroyed Alan and he never forgave his son. Later Christopher said he regretted it and admitted his own bitterness 'had overflowed more publicly than it should have done'. He said in the piece:

Ever since I was quite a small boy, I have hated being
Christopher Robin.
My father had as little to do with children as possible. I was
his only child and I lived upstairs in the nursery. I saw very
little of him. It was my mother who used to come and play in
the nursery with me and tell him about the things I thought and
did. It was she who provided most of the material for my
father's books.

Asked about his famous bedtime stories, Christopher added: 'I had one installment every evening, but I never remember *Winnie-the-Pooh* being brought into them.'

But he did at least manage to find a few less hostile things to say when it came to memories of Alan being home to teach him cricket and algebra. He went on:

I was always very grateful to him for being so good at admiring anything I did make – however hideous it might be. He once put up an almost useless bright blue wall-bracket in his bedroom just because I had made it. He was a good father to me although it wasn't until I was twelve that we really came to know each other well. Instead of writing poems about me, he started writing amusing letters to me. He taught me to play golf – that was rather more successful than cricket. Today he is very ill in hospital and I am grown up. I shall never get over my dislike of being "the real live Christopher Robin". But when I sell one of my father's books in the bookshop I own, I can't help feeling a little proud of him.

Christopher had been told that his father only had days left to live, and presumably gave the interview believing that he would never know what he said. When the article appeared, Daphne was mortified at the public humiliation, and tried to keep it hidden from Alan, who was being nursed around the clock. But he was told all about it by a well-meaning friend who made it sound so horrendous that Alan took the dramatic step of changing his will. Whatever alterations he may or may not have made at the time – and there is no question that Alan absolutely hated the article – Christopher's inheritance remained very substantial indeed.

Alan's strength gradually returned, and as he started to show signs of improvement, medical experts decided he was well enough to risk an operation on his brain at the end of December. Doctors warned Daphne that the surgery would be 'kill or cure', but it was neither. It left him alive but in a worse condition than before, and partly paralysed. For the rest of his life he was confined to a wheelchair, although he could still speak and write a little. He longed to return to Cotchford, and on 27 January he was allowed to move a little closer, to convalesce at a nursing home in Tunbridge Wells.

CHAPTER SIXTEEN

According to Christopher, after the operation his father became a very different man, people could not help noticing the dramatic and distressing change in Alan's character and personality. Gone was the mild-mannered gentleman and in his place appeared someone coarse, vulgar, irritable, and perverse, traits which certainly had not been there before: 'If it is sad to go too soon, it is worse to stay too long,' said Christopher who only saw his father twice during the three years that he was gravely ill.

Most of us have small, sad places somewhere in our hearts and my father was no exception, Christopher wrote. *Sometimes we let our feelings escape in bursts of anger. Sometimes we make long, dismal faces. My father did neither. He felt deeply but kept his feelings to himself. Or rather, being a writer, he let them escape in his writing. But even here he disguised them, unable even in fiction to allow himself to take himself too seriously. If the sad side of my father's life was kept from me as a child, I shall not now try to unearth it. Enough for me to be grateful that I knew only his smiles.*

Alan's heart had been shattered by Christopher's humiliating newspaper interview, and he remained furious with his son until the day he died. He was still angry two years after it was published, when he mentioned it in a letter he struggled to write to Maud. The handwriting is almost unrecognisable, and it is believed to be the last of many hundreds of letters he had sent his sister-in-law in the years since he promised Ken he would always take care of her.

Did you read Moon's article on me in the Sunday Dispatch when I was supposed to be dying? he asked her. *You'd have been disgusted. Oh well, I lost him years ago, but I still have Daff. Thank God, though I give her a rotten time I'm afraid. But from 11.30-1.30 we are out in the garden together, doing the Times Xword at lunch-time – the high spot of my day. My hand and eyes are getting tired – so I must stop.*

In the same letter he thanked Maud and her family for sending about 150 letters, for which I am very grateful and for your patience.

Daphne was not the only one being given 'a rotten time', Alan was a terrible patient and none of the nurses sent to care for him lasted very long at all. He was physically frail but seemed to scare them all away. He told Maud how yet another nurse, called Monty, had recently left:

> *Of course life with me goes on much the same since the departure of the famous Monty (I must have told you about him as I had him for ten months – real name Worthington, and the son of a Colonel...) – one impossibly foul or incompetent nurse after another; until a month ago when we got an absolute toot called Campbell, very Scottish, says "Wee Willie" all day long. I told him that if he said it more than twenty-five times a day, I'd brain him. He just laughs. All the others would have given twenty-four hours' notice on the spot. I can say what I like to him and he knows I'm not serious. Wonderful in a Scotsman. But a funny story or a limerick leaves him absolutely blank.*

This nurse, J.G. Campbell, nicknamed Daphne 'the bloody Duchess' but was so fond of Alan that he agreed to witness the changes he decided to make to his will. The second witness was his physiotherapist Joan M. Fuller who spent much of those final months at Alan's side. She was hired to visit Alan at home three or four times a week, but came to dislike and dread those appointments at Cotchford. She described Alan as 'sad, sour, bitter and bored to tears'. He would summon her for sessions, even at weekends and on Bank Holidays, simply for a diversion in the long and awful emptiness of his days. Joan also noticed that Daphne 'couldn't handle illness,' and although Alan criticised everyone and everything else, he would never say a word against his wife: 'How beautiful she is,' he once remarked to Joan with tears in his eyes.

For Christmas 1953 he presented Joan with a copy of *Year In, Year Out*, with the message: 'Gratefully and in the hope of improving her mind.' And the following year he gave her a first edition of *The Pocket Milne*, this time admitting how rude and grumpy he had been to her in his inscription:

> *For Joan Fuller (aged 23)*
> *First prize for*
> *Punctuality*
> *Neatness*
> *Physiotherapy*
> *And*
> *Imperviousness to Insults*
> *From*
> *A.A. Milne*
> *Christmas Term, 1954.*

Despite the many months she spent with him Joan remembered Alan only mentioning Christopher once, on Good Friday the year before he died, when he remarked sadly: 'We have *all* given our only sons.'

In February 1954 Alan was persuaded by Daphne to host one last party in London. It was the sort of thing he had avoided for some years but *The Times* reported how an ambulance had taken him to Brown's Hotel, his old haunt where many of his friends gathered:

> *Mr Milne in 1952 underwent a severe operation on the brain; he has since been partly paralysed and unable to walk. This year he wished to repeat for his friends the party he used to give annually. Mr Milne received the guests in a chair and was later driven back to his home at Hartfield, Sussex.*

It was a sad and uncomfortable occasion, as he had put on a huge amount of weight, was stuck in his wheelchair, and virtually unrecognisable to most of his guests. They all felt sorry to see the state he was in: 'He was not my A.A.M. anymore,' said his niece Angela. That was the last time his nieces would see their beloved uncle as Daphne could not cope with visitors at Cotchford. When Marjorie asked if she could come down the reply she received was a terse: 'We are not a normal household.'

The party in London took a heavy toll on Alan's health, and three weeks later he was seriously ill again, struck down with a bout of pneumonia and rushed back to the Lonsdale Nursing Home in Tunbridge Wells. The outlook was dire but he defied doctors, and survived yet another setback. By April he was allowed to return to Cotchford, but even his old adversaries were worried about his failing health. P.G. Wodehouse who had clearly forgotten how much he had once longed for Alan 'to break his bloody neck', wrote a letter from his mansion on Long Island to a friend called Alistair Wallace, expressing great sympathy for his fellow writer:

Poor Milne. I was shocked to hear of his illness. I'm afraid there seems very little chance of him getting any better. It is ghastly to think of anyone who wrote such gay stuff ending his life like this. He has always been about my favourite author. I have all his books and re-read them regularly.

Alan was stable, but showing no signs of improvement, although clearly he was not a man to go quietly without a fight. He still had the strength to get himself worked up about what he read in the newspapers each morning, and remarkably he had another letter to *The Times* in him. His final contribution was on the question of subsidiary rights in books, a subject which had been enraging him for at least the past twenty-five years:

The president of the Booksellers Association ought to know better than to trot out yet once again the ineffably silly argument that "nine out of 10 authors would not stand the slightest chance of having their books filmed, dramatised, broadcast etc, unless they had first been published", and, that therefore the publisher is entitled to a share in the loot, he wrote. It would be just as sensible to say that their books would not even have been read by a publisher if they had not been typed and that therefore the typist was entitled to a share in the author's royalties. All sorts of odd honours come the way of the successful author. He is knighted (if he likes that sort of thing), invited to country houses, asked to make speeches, give away prizes etc. Does he always take his publisher with him, saying to the Lord Chamberlain, his hostess or the headmaster of his country school, "I hope you don't mind me bringing old Prendergast along. You see, he's my publisher, and but for him you would never have heard of me."

One last remark: Mr Page seems to have overlooked the fact that it is nearly always the successful books that get etcetered, and that if they are successful the publishers have made their profit – probably more than the author. And I might add that no publisher has yet shown the slightest sign of being an experienced literary, dramatic and film agent.

Alan could still string together a decent argument when it came to matters he was passionate about, but there was no denying that he had lost much of his appetite for life. His final eighteen months were dreary and empty, he barely left the house and refused to see anyone. Daphne helped nurse him around the clock and Christmas 1955 was bleak and lonely for them both. They were invited to a new production of *Toad of Toad Hall*, starring Leo McKern in the lead role, and Daphne was keen for a change of scenery, but Alan could not muster the strength to take an interest.

Shortly after the New Year he slipped gently into unconsciousness and on 31 January 1956, Alan died at the age 74. Marjorie vividly remembered the moment she heard of her uncle's death, which made headlines on the BBC's eight o'clock news. It was also her brother Tony's birthday, and moments later Daphne phoned and they consoled one another. The cause of death on the official certificate was given as 'Cerebro vascular degeneration, Brain abscess and Pneumonia'.

A well-attended Memorial Service was held for Alan on 10 February at All Hallows by the Tower Church in London. The actor Nicholas Hannen, who had appeared in *The Dover Road* some forty-four years earlier, read the poem *Let Us Now Praise Famous Men*, while Kenneth Bird from *Punch* read the passage from St Mark: 'Suffer the little children to come unto me, and forbid them not; for of such is the Kingdom of God.'

Alan's friend Norman Shelley sang Pooh's song *How Sweet To Be A Cloud* and recited *Vespers* to an organ accompaniment. Christopher was there but his wife Lesley did not travel from Devon for the service, using the excuse that she was six months pregnant at the time and did not feel well enough to make the long journey. Daphne was dismayed when Christopher turned up in a scruffy old overcoat, they barely spoke and never saw each other again after that day, although Daphne went on to live another fifteen years. Afterwards Daphne explained how upset she had been at seeing her estranged son in a letter she wrote to Maud following the funeral, at which she appeared to have been medicated to calm her nerves:

It was rather shattering that my so-called steadying 'dope' seemed to lose its effect at the critical moment when I needed it most! And I was completely overcome at the end of the service (and with no opportunity of even powdering my nose before meeting people!) I, too, felt the service was perfect and just what Blue would have liked.

It is not recorded how Christopher must have felt hearing Norman Shelley recite *Vespers*, which he called 'that wretched poem' and blamed for starting all of his problems with bullying, stuttering and ultimately the bitter fall out with his father which could never be resolved: 'It is one of my father's best known and one that has brought me over the years more toe-curling, fist-clenching, lip-biting embarrassment than any other,' Christopher said.

There were many glowing obituaries following Alan's death of course, but he would have been disappointed to see that they focused almost entirely on *The House at Pooh Corner* and the three other children's books, which by this stage had topped more than seven million in worldwide sales. The best-selling American magazine *Time* devoted several pages to a posthumous feature which said:

CHAPTER SIXTEEN

*In the closing words of his last children's book, A.A. Milne
unintentionally summed up his own claim to immortality.
"Wherever they go," he said of Pooh and Christopher Robin,
"and whatever happens to them on the way, in that enchanted
place on the top of the Forest a little boy and his bear will
always be playing."*

When Cotchford was sold following Daphne's death in 1971,
Christopher did not keep any of his parent's belongings apart from two
old jars that Alan used to keep a supply of green mint flavoured sweets
in, and would they both take one to finish every meal:

One thing only I kept as a reminder, Christopher said. *The pair
of jars that had housed the Green Sweets since before I was
born. Somewhere inside them was locked away the secret of the
happiness they gave. I shall never discover it. I don't want to
learn it. It is enough to look at them from time to time and know
that it is there.*

The farm was bought by rock star Brian Jones, a founding member of
The Rolling Stones, but within a year he was discovered dead at the
bottom of the swimming pool. From then on controversy surrounded
the six-bedroom house, which dates back to the sixteenth century, as
there were rumours that Jones had been murdered. Keith Richards,
who always referred to the place as 'Winnie-the-Pooh's house' wrote
in his autobiography how the band's disgruntled minder Frank
Thorogood, who had been fired that day, made a deathbed confession
that he drowned Jones. Recently the property, which still has a statue
of Christopher Robin in the garden, was back on the market for the
first time in more than forty years, with an asking price of £1.9m. The
charming village of Hartfield has become an enormously popular
tourist attraction, where every year thousands of visitors flock to see
landmarks including Pooh Corner, the Hundred Acre Wood, Galleon's
Lap, and of course to play games of Poohsticks on the famous bridge.

Christopher continued to shy away from journalists and a curious public asking endless questions about his childhood, but finally in 1974 he decided it was time to lay some of those ghosts to rest and the result was his first autobiography, *The Enchanted Places*. He dedicated it to Olive Brockwell, his former nanny known as Nou, saying: 'To remind you of those enchanted places, where the past will always be present.' Alan and Daphne's worst fears were realised when their only grandchild, Christopher and Lesley's daughter Clare, was born severely disabled, suffering badly from cerebral palsy and a number of other rare debilitating conditions which affected the connection between the brain and the muscles and meaning she had to spend most of her life receiving intensive care. The Clare Milne Trust was set up in 2002, helping others suffering from similar conditions. Using Christopher's share of Alan's royalties, the aim of the charity is to help people with disabilities in Devon and Cornwall. But her mother explained that her late grandfather's money meant nothing to Clare: 'She's rather vague about that sort of thing,' Lesley said. 'She doesn't know the difference between £1,000 and £10,000. That's rather nice, don't you think?'

Clare died in 2012, by which time Christopher's health was poor too. After suffering badly for many years from the neuromuscular disease myasthenia gravis, he died in his sleep 1996 at the age of 75, and Lesley passed away in 2014.

Very few of Alan's plays for adults would be remembered after he was gone, and by the time he died most of his adult novels and poems had long been out of print too. But each year, in an ever-increasing multitude of languages, those 70,000 words that he wrote for children continue to sell in their millions and smash all previous publishing records. In 1960 a Latin version, called *Winnie ille Pu* sold 100,000 copies in record time and became the first book in a foreign language to become an American bestseller.

With constantly rising worldwide sales, the books are still being sold every day in eighty-six countries, having been translated into more than fifty languages, including Chinese, Japanese, Croatian, Serbian, Latvian, Icelandic and even Esperanto. In Russia, where he is known as *Vinni Pukh*, Pooh is vastly popular.

Fans were stunned in 2009 when news broke that there would at last be long-awaited sequel to Alan's stories. On the last page of *The House at Poor Corner*, Christopher was due to go to boarding school, leaving the inhabitants of the Hundred Acre Wood to continue their adventures alone. Author David Benedictus was given the daunting task of writing an authorised update. Luckily he shared Alan's great sense of humour and, showing how very aware he was of the risk he was taking, Benedictus wrote in the new book: "'But are you really going to write us new adventures?" Christopher Robin asks. "Because we rather liked the old ones."' A sentence or so later Eeyore gives his thoughts – and, unsurprisingly, they are not encouraging. "'He'll get it wrong" says Eeyore, "see if he doesn't. What does he know about donkeys?"'

The pressure was immense, but to Benedictus' enormous relief, the Trustees of the Pooh Properties, who represent both the Milne and Shepard estates, had high praise for the sequel, saying that the ten new short stories had 'captured the spirit and quality of those original books'. David Riley, director of Egmont Publishing, said: '*Return to the Hundred Acre Wood* is set to be a huge hit this year with children and parents alike. We are delighted to be publishing the sequel to a wonderful children's classic.'

Martyn Luke, head of marketing and brands, added that the tales were 'very faithful' to the original: 'It's our biggest launch of the year and some people are saying it's going to be the publishing event of the year,' he said. 'Because of the popularity of Pooh it really does have a huge age range appeal.'

The rights to the characters were sold to Disney in 1961 and boosted profits for the US conglomerate more than anyone could have predicted. Alan knew Pooh was popular but he had no idea the vast scale of what imagination had created. Disney merchandise sales still continue to rake in an astonishing $3 billion a year today and rising – second only to Mickey Mouse. In 1966, Disney artists animated a *Pooh* story for the first time, called *Winnie The Pooh And The Honey Tree*. It smashed box office records, and scores of films and television adaptations have followed, although they have been fiercely criticised.

The multi-billion dollar franchise came under fire from many of Alan's most die-hard fans who felt they were not true enough to the original stories – particularly as the characters were given American accents. E.H. Shepard blasted the first film as 'a complete travesty'. But they dramatically increased global awareness and did absolutely nothing to diminish sales of the books, which continue to soar to this day.

In 2016 another big budget Hollywood film called *Goodbye Christopher Robin* went into production, exploring the controversial relationship between Alan and his son, starring Domnhall Gleeson as Alan and Margot Robbie playing Daphne. According to the production company Fox Searchlight Pictures, the eagerly awaited movie will provide:

A rare glimpse into the relationship between beloved children's author A. A. Milne and his son Christopher Robin, whose toys inspired the magical world of Winnie the Pooh. Along with his mother Daphne, and his nanny Olive, Christopher Robin and his family are swept up in the international success of the books; the enchanting tales bringing hope and comfort to England after the First World War. But with the eyes of the world on Christopher Robin, what will the cost be to the family?

Director Simon Curtis added: 'I am delighted to be collaborating with screen writer Frank Cottrell Boyce to tell the remarkable and poignant story of the family behind the creation of *Winnie-the-Pooh*.'

In 2014 *Winnie-the-Pooh* was named the best-loved children's book of the last 150 years, pushing even Lewis Carroll's *Alice's Adventures in Wonderland*, written in 1865, into second place for the first time, in the poll of thousands of adults. It also beat children's classics including *The Hobbit* and *The Gruffalo*.

Alan may have fought it tooth and nail, but his delightful creations are deeply entrenched in our culture even now. It is taken for granted that people will instantly know precisely what 'behaving like Tigger' or 'sounding like Eeyore' means. The stories remain much loved and cherished by world leaders, philosophers, and business gurus, and there are still no better books for sharing between parents and their children. And there can be no doubt they will capture the imaginations of many generations to come.

It may have not been in the way he wanted, but through them Alan achieved immortality. Shortly after *Winnie-the-Pooh* was first published back in 1926 he wrote: 'I suppose that every one of us hopes secretly for immortality; to leave, I mean, a name behind him which will live forever in this world, whatever he may be doing, himself, in the next.'

Bibliography

Milne A.A. *Michael and Mary* (Chatto & Windus London, 1930)

Milne A.A. *Peace With Honour* (E.P. Dutton & Co. 1934)

Milne A.A. *The House At Pooh Corner* (Methuen & Co. London, 1928)

Milne A.A. *Toad of Toad Hall* (Samuel French, 1929)

Milne A.A. *Winnie-The-Pooh* (Methuen & Co. London, 1926)

Milne A.A. *When We Were Very Young* (Methuen & Co. London, 1924)

Milne A.A. *Year In, Year Out* (Methuen & Co. London, 1952)

Milne C., *The Enchanted Places* (Methuen Books London, 1974)

Milne C., *The Path Through The Trees* (Pan Macmillan London, 1983)

Thwaite A., *A.A. Milne His Life* (Faber and Faber London, 1990)

Archive: *New York Post.* Review of Milne's works. (New York)

Archive*: The Observer.* Review of Milne's works. (London)

Archive*: The Telegraph.* Letter sent from Milne. (London)

Archive*: The Times.* Letter sent from Milne. (London)